Joseph Smith's Tritheism

Joseph Smith's Tritheism

The Prophet's Theology in Historical Context,
Critiqued from a Nicene Perspective

Dayton Hartman

WIPF & STOCK · Eugene, Oregon

JOSEPH SMITH'S TRITHEISM
The Prophet's Theology in Historical Context, Critiqued from a Nicene Perspective

Wipf & Stock
An Imprint of Wipf and Stock Publishers
199 W. 8th Ave., Suite 3
Eugene, OR 97401

www.wipfandstock.com

ISBN 13: 978-1-4982-6812-7

Manufactured in the U.S.A.

Contents

Acknowledgments

Without the input, guidance, encouragement, and contributions of numerous individuals, this project would have never come to fruition. I cannot begin to express the depth of my gratitude to those who have tirelessly supported me throughout the writing and compiling of this research. I will briefly mention those individuals who have been most critical in the completion of this research.

First, I must thank those who guided me in my Ph.D. research (much of which undergirds this book), Professors Daniel Lioy and Andries le R. du Plooy. Their scholarly feedback has been priceless. Second, my dear wife, Rebekah, spent countless hours supporting me in this research and acting as one of my editors. Without her love, encouragement, and editorial input, I could not have finished this program. Third, my son Jude deserves mentioning. It was after my wife and I learned that we would be having our first child that I was inspired to undertake doctoral studies, which led to the production of this book. Fourth, I must express my immense gratitude to Dr. Winfried Corduan for acting as my copyeditor. His ability to think as an editor, historian, theologian, and philosopher has been an answer to prayer.

Abbreviations

Jas.	James
Joh.	*Commentary on the Gospel According to John*
Judg.	Judges
I Kgs.	I Kings
Lev.	Leviticus
Mag.	Letter to the Magnesians
Matt.	Matthew
NICNT	*New International Commentary on the New Testament*
Num.	Numbers
I Pet.	I Peter
II Pet.	II Peter
Phil.	Philippians
Phlm.	Philemon
Plea.	A Plea for the Christians
Prax.	Against Praxeas
Princ.	On First Principles
Ps.	Psalms
Rev.	Revelation
Rom.	Romans
I Sam.	I Samuel
I Thess.	I Thessalonians
II Thess.	II Thessalonians
I Tim.	I Timothy
II Tim.	II Timothy
Tres dii.	On Not Three Gods
Trin.	On the Holy Trinity

Chapter 1

Introduction

BACKGROUND

For nearly two thousand years, the doctrine of the Trinity has stood at the center of theological orthodoxy. Based upon the text of enscripturated revelation and in accordance with the rule of faith, Christians have historically recognized the triune nature of God,[1] while at the same time holding firm to Abrahamic monotheism.[2] In North America, this doctrine was firmly established in the beliefs of those who migrated to the New World in hopes of enjoying religious freedom. What developed, particularly in the Northeastern portion of the American Colonies, was a historically orthodox, theological stronghold.[3] Doctrinally, a great deal of homogeny existed among the colonies. While there certainly were theological nuances from sect to sect, there was a general adherence to theological essentials that had historically defined the Christian faith, including the doctrine of the Trinity.

Mark Noll demonstrates that during the late eighteenth and early nineteenth centuries, a drift away from established orthodoxy began to occur, particularly in the Northeast of the American Colonies.[4] Even though Noll provides a well-written and meticulously researched account of this

---

1. Kelly, *Early Christian Doctrines*, 95.
2. Horrell, "The Eternal Son of God in the Social Trinity," 45.
3. Noll, *America's God*, 3–52.
4. Ibid., 66.

1

theological drift, he does not adequately discuss the resulting unorthodox movements that arose due to this theological innovation. Such information is critical because it was during this time period that the orthodox denominations witnessed a significant falling away of members.[5] The abandonment of traditional orthodoxy must be connected to the rise of anti-orthodox attitudes and the movements these sentiments birthed.

A number of the organized movements that departed from orthodoxy arose or settled near Palmyra, New York: the same town that gave rise to the North American tritheism known as Mormonism.[6] Ruth Tucker's historical survey of New Religions, particularly in North America, provides relevant data for understanding the rise of unorthodox movements, yet it does not go far enough in examining the varying influences and motives that led to the splitting away from orthodoxy. The general mood of the colonies in the Northeast was that of freedom in theological exploration and invention, an attitude somewhat resulting from the millennial fervor that had arisen around the time of the American Revolution.[7] Interest in millennial apocalyptic religion, regardless of its orthodoxy, had become en vogue. Surprisingly, this factor has yet to be considered as one of numerous influences leading to the eventual rise of North American tritheism. In the nearly two centuries since the time of Joseph Smith, Mormonism's adherents have remained true to its nuanced and seemingly ever-changing position on the nature of the Godhead. While undertaking clarifications over time, the central element of Smith's theology, tritheism, has remained intact.[8]

Two resources, in particular, stand out as excellent accounts of Joseph Smith's early life, as well as his prophetic career. First, from an evangelical perspective, *One Nation Under Gods* (2003) proves a valuable resource in understanding early Mormonism. Richard Abanes depicts the questionable character of Joseph Smith in both his business life and his role as a self-proclaimed prophet. However, *One Nation Under Gods* does not situate Smith's divergence from historical orthodoxy in its proper context. The book supplies little information to acquaint the reader with the theological climate of the Northeast during and just preceding Smith's lifetime. Historian and LDS adherent Richard Bushman's account of Smith's life, *Joseph*

---

5. Finke and Stark, *The Churching of America 1776–1990*, 54–59.

6. Tucker, *Another Gospel*, 41.

7. Hatch, "The Origins of Civil Millennialism in America," 87.

8. McConkie, *Mormon Doctrine*, 319.

Smith: Rough Stone Rolling (2007), has become the standard for a modern recounting of Mormonism's founding prophet's life from a perspective that is sympathetic to the LDS church. While providing an exceptional portrait of the historical and cultural context in which Mormonism was born, Bushman proves to be unsuccessful in his effort to provide the reader with the necessary understanding of the theological context in which Smith began teaching his unique understanding of God.

PROBLEM STATEMENT

Asserting that Smith restored true doctrine, LDS adherents fail to recognize that Smith was just one of many voices advocating a departure from Christian orthodoxy.[9] Joseph Smith proposed, contrary to Nicene orthodoxy, that there is not one God, but that there are many gods. However, the gods that are to be worshipped are the three gods who act with one purpose.[10] Rather than attempting a reformulation of historic Trinitarian Christianity, Smith envisioned a theological system meant to replace historic Nicene Christianity.[11] Since the time of Joseph Smith, Mormonism has continued to contour itself to the historical context in which it exists. The doctrinal formulations found within early Mormonism have changed over decades, resulting in modern LDS doctrinal explanations, which remain staunchly tritheistic.[12] Modern LDS apologists continue to attack historic Nicene orthodoxy as unbiblical, insisting instead upon Smith's unique tritheistic understanding of God.[13] Orthodox Christianity should respond by defining its parameters, rooted in an exegesis of the Scriptures, and maintained by what has been held as the rule of faith since the time of the early church.

CENTRAL RESEARCH QUESTION

The central theoretical question of this work, therefore, is: What was the theological context in which Joseph Smith diverged from Nicene orthodoxy,

9. Tucker, *Another Gospel*, 40.

10. Smith, *Teachings of the Prophet Joseph Smith*, 370.

11. Blomberg and Robinson, *How Wide the Divide?*, 132; Millet and McDermott, *Claiming Christ*, 78.

12. Peterson and Ricks, "Comparing LDS Beliefs with First-Century Christianity," 7.

13. Hopkins, *Biblical Mormonism*, 51–108.

and, given his divergence, how should Nicene Trinitarian orthodoxy respond to and criticize Joseph Smith's tritheism?

The questions that emerge from this problem include:

- What is the clear, systematic teaching of Scripture regarding the nature of God?

- What is the historical, orthodox position on the Trinity, and how early was it established?

- How is the doctrine of the Trinity currently being addressed among orthodox theologians?

- What was the historical context in which Joseph Smith formulated his tritheism?

- In what manner did Joseph Smith's theological environment encourage theological innovation?

- How has Smith's doctrine of God been revised or clarified by LDS leadership over nearly two centuries into its modern expression?

- How should orthodox, Nicene Christianity approach and criticize Smith's (and the modern LDS) doctrine of God?

THE AIM AND OBJECTIVES

The aim of this research is to establish the historical context in which Joseph Smith formulated his tritheism, to examine innovations and clarifications of LDS tritheism, and to provide an evaluation and critique of Smith's tritheism from the perspective of Nicene Christianity.

The objectives of this study are seen in relationship to the aim. We will approach this subject from the following angles: first, identify the core elements of historic, creedal Trinitarianism rooted in the Canon of Scripture and upheld through the rule of faith. Second, engage with the text of Scripture, using sound rules of exegesis, to identify the biblical teaching on the doctrine of the Trinity. Third, explore the religious, historical context in which Joseph Smith developed his tritheism and its implications for theological departure from orthodoxy. Fourth, recount major innovations, clarification, and expansions upon Joseph Smith's tritheism that have culminated in current LDS doctrine. Firth, utilize the core elements of creedal Trinitarianism, rooted in a correct exegesis of the Scriptures and upheld by the rule of faith, to evaluate and criticize Smith's theology, as well as current LDS doctrine, regarding the nature of God.

METHODOLOGY

This research will employ a careful consideration of relevant data necessary for the proper formulation of a conclusion. Data providing the theological context of late eighteenth and early nineteenth centuries will be examined using studies that engage with the broad spectrum of North American religious history,[14] works focused upon eighteenth century theology,[15] as well as revivalism[16] among early North American evangelicals. This approach is necessary to produce a clear, theological context in which to understand Joseph Smith's sense of doctrinal freedom. This inquiry further necessitates an interaction with LDS sources recounting the life of Joseph Smith (e.g., Bushman). Due to Smith's claim that his theology was a restoration of early Christian doctrine, a thorough study of early church Trinitarianism must be undertaken. This study will utilize modern works analyzing early Christian beliefs including standard works such as *Early Christian Doctrines*,[17] *The Emergence of Catholic Tradition*,[18] and *The History of Christian Doctrine*.[19] Further, consideration will be afforded to specialized texts focusing upon the development of Nicene orthodoxy. These sources include *Nicaea and its Legacy*[20] and *The Search for the Christian Doctrine of God*.[21] In terms of primary source texts from the early church fathers, ante-Nicene, Nicene, and post-Nicene will be explored. This exploration must also engage with early church commentaries on Scripture.

Due to the rootedness of Trinitarianism in the text of Scripture, adequate attention will be given to hermeneutical matters, lexical issues, and exegetical approaches, resulting in a biblical-theological definition of the Trinity. By examining early church history and relying upon the proper

---

14. Sweet, *The Story of Religion in America*.

15. Noll, *America's God*.

16. Wolffe, *The Expansion of Evangelicalism*.

17. Kelly, 1960.

18. Pelikan, 1975.

19. Berkhof, 1996.

20. Ayers, 2006.

21. Hanson, 2006.

interpretation of Scripture, resulting creedal and theological formulations will be used as the lens by which to criticize Smith's tritheism.

Admittedly, this author approaches the data as a committed evangelical from the Reformed tradition. Therefore, the goal will be to utilize a variety of sources not written by those sharing the same theological tradition. While such sources will not be used exclusively, their argumentation will be carefully considered. The purpose of using sources from varying traditions is an attempt to disengage, as much as possible, from the aforementioned theological bias and to allow the data uncovered in this research to speak for itself.

In summary, intending to explore all perspectives and avenues of information in this research, the following methods will be employed:

- Primary source research as to what historically constituted orthodox, Christian doctrine as it relates to the nature of the Godhead. For the sake of being succinct, this research will be limited to the first four hundred years of church history;

- an examination of the historical progression of orthodoxy in North America and the eventual splintering of orthodoxy into sectarian groups within the Northeast colonies in the eighteenth and nineteenth centuries;

- a thorough study of first-hand LDS and non-LDS sources that provide an account of Joseph Smith's life and thought;

- recounting the expansions upon, clarifications of and innovations in restating Smith's tritheism through history into modern LDS doctrine by utilizing LDS documents;

- an examination Smith's theology (and modern LDS doctrine) in light of historic creedal Trinitarianism, a clear exegesis of the text of Scripture, and the rule of faith.

CONTENT OVERVIEW

Over the past two hundred years, much has been written on Mormonism and its founding prophet, Joseph Smith. The research presented in this project will attempt to further engage Joseph Smith's theology (and, by proxy, Mormonism as a whole) by delving into the historic content of biblical orthodoxy in distinction to the teachings of the LDS Church. Before charting the course that lies ahead, it is only prudent to disclose the limitations of this project.

First, some writers have ventured to systematize the content of LDS theology before engaging with the particulars. In order to accomplish the aim of this research, such a method will not be attempted. Second, when assessing the life and theology of Joseph Smith, there has been a tendency to focus upon the moral failures of the Smith family as a whole. While some of this material will certainly be broached in this work, there will be no attempt to explain or disclose every flaw in the general character of the Smith family. Last, the current apologetic nuances of LDS scholarship will not be criticized beyond what is necessary for this research.

The course that will be taken will be an integrated approach to key elements of historic orthodoxy. In chapter 2, the case for Trinitarianism based upon the content of the Scriptures[22] will be advanced. This will by no means be an exhaustive account of every element of biblical text pointing to the triunity of the Godhead. However, key Trinitarian texts will be considered both contextually and exegetically. Chapter 3 will trace the clarification of Trinitarian theology through its first few centuries of exposition. Given that the current trend in popular non-Christian works is to portray the doctrine of the Trinity as ad hoc theology conceived numerous centuries after the life of Christ, an exploration of early church fathers will prove significantly useful in clarifying Trinitarian development. Moving from the early church proper, chapter 4 will center on the early North American church. It will be demonstrated that the early church in North America was both dynamic and yet largely orthodox. However, what began as an orthodox institution quickly trended towards unorthodox theological explorations as the eighteenth century drew to a close. Furthermore, Joseph Smith's theological development and influences will be evaluated. The data examined will establish that Joseph Smith's theology developed through an evolutionary process borne out of context and necessity. Chapter 5 will seek to trace the clarifications and modern theological innovations in LDS tritheism from the time of Joseph Smith to the modern era. This information will be followed by an assessment of Smith's tritheism from a Nicene perspective. Finally, chapter 6 will supply a cohesive conclusion to the content presented throughout this project. Additionally, areas of research necessitating further study will be noted.

22. Unless otherwise noted, all references to the Christian Scriptures are taken from the *English Standard Version*, 2001.

Chapter 2

The Trinity in the Scriptures

INTRODUCTION

Nicene orthodoxy is Trinitarianism, and Trinitarianism is Nicene orthodoxy. Such a statement immediately brings to mind a critical question: What is the basis of Nicene orthodoxy? Is it, as some LDS apologists[1] claim, pagan philosophy? The answer to such a question should come in two parts.

First, philosophical categories utilized by pagan philosophers have been employed to express the doctrine of the Trinity. Yet, this usage does not make the doctrine any less true. To discount the value of certain descriptive linguistic categories due to their usage by pagan peoples would render virtually all language unusable. Further, even LDS scholar Robert Millet admits that pagan language and philosophical concepts are employed in the bounds of Mormon theology.[2]

The second step in answering the above question requires the attention of this chapter. Even if pagan philosophical categories have been utilized in describing the doctrine of the Trinity, this does not make the doctrine invalid if the basis for the doctrine is grounded in God's self-revelation. Provided that the foundation for Nicene orthodoxy can be found within the text of enscripturated revelation, the goal of the expositor of Scripture is to accurately describe what is represented in God's self-revelation, regardless

---

1. Oaks, "Apostasy and Restoration," 84.
2. Millet, "The Eternal Gospel," 48.

of the heritage of linguistic categories necessary to convey what is taught in Scripture.

Therefore, the purpose of this chapter will be to examine the grounding of Nicene orthodoxy: the Scriptures. This is necessary to answer one of the secondary research questions central to the purpose of this project. That secondary question is simply this: What is the clear, systematic teaching of Scripture regarding the doctrine of the Trinity? A mere sampling of two or three key Trinitarian passages will not suffice in establishing a case for Trinitarian teaching within the text of Scripture. From the Nicene perspective, the Trinity is revealed in the pervasive and consistent manner in which the persons of the Godhead are mentioned throughout the entirety of Scripture.[3] What must be seen is the overall arc of Trinitarian theology demonstrated in Scripture as a whole.

The course taken through this chapter will first necessitate the establishment of monotheism as foundational to Nicene Trinitarianism. However, merely listing or engaging with texts that indicate monotheism in the Old Testament will not adequately detail the theological background for Nicene Trinitarianism, given the contemporary trend to interpret early Israelite monotheism as henotheism. Therefore, a fair amount of attention will be dedicated to the issues of monotheism versus henotheism in the Old Testament. Moving forward, allusions to the Trinity within the text of the Old Testament will receive consideration. This will provide the reader with the traditional, Nicene interpretation of plurality allusions within the Old Testament. However, the bulk of the research in this chapter will center upon the Trinitarian data revealed in the scriptural portrayal of Father, Son, and Spirit as all divine persons. The chapter will then conclude with a summary of Triadic formulations found throughout the text of the New Testament.

THE BASIS OF THE TRINITY: MONOTHEISM

The most important Old Testament text regarding the uniqueness of God is found within the confession of Hebrew monotheism, the *Shema*. The passage from which the *Shema* is taken, Deut. 6:4, reads "Hear, O Israel! The LORD is our God, the LORD is one!" The Hebrew word used in this text for "one" is *'echad*. Even though the word is accurately translated as "one," it

---

3. McGrath, *Christian Theology: An Introduction*, 248.

does not imply a position of isolation.[4] Instead, 'echad stresses the uniqueness, as well as the unity, of *Yahweh*.[5] In John Sailhamer's opinion, the intent of the passage is to provide a clear distinction between the monotheism of Israel and the polytheism of the surrounding nations.[6] William Dyrness concurs with Sailhamer's argument. Although Dyrness believes that the early Old Testament data demonstrate a commitment by the patriarchs to monolatry rather than monotheism, he sees the *Shema* as a statement of absolute monotheism.[7] In his view, regardless of the somewhat debatable nature of the theology of the patriarchs, the *Shema* does appear to teach that there is but one being that can be qualitatively described as God.

Despite taking a rather critical approach to the text of Deuteronomy, Alexander Rofe concludes that the context of this passage has to be understood in light of the Ancient Near Eastern (henceforth referred to as ANE) belief in regional gods.[8] Yet, as Rofe argues, the *Shema* must be acknowledged as a condemnation of other gods for not being gods at all.[9] This approach seems to provide a balanced and canonical understanding of the Old Testament assertions that *Yahweh* alone is God, but men serve "strange" gods. Approaching the issue from the opposite end of the theological spectrum, Todd Miles comes to a similar conclusion regarding the *Shema* when he writes:

> Fundamental to Old Testament monotheism is not merely the explicit denial of other "gods," though such denials are there. . .Rather, the Israelite people were to worship the Lord God who is essentially and categorically different from any other being, whether real or imagined, natural or supernatural, who was worshipped as "god" by the surrounding peoples.[10]

In the end, both Rofe and Miles conclude that the *Shema* teaches that there is not just one true God of Israel, but also of the entire universe.[11] The

---

4. Mounce, *Mounce's Complete Expository dictionary of Old Testament and New Testament Words*, 485.

5. Sailhamer, *The Pentateuch as Narrative*, 439.

6. Ibid.

7. Dyrness, *Themes in Old Testament Theology*, 48.

8. Rofe, *Old Testament Studies: Deuteronomy*, 19.

9. Ibid.

10. Miles, *A God of Many Understandings?*, 51–52.

11. Rofe, *Old Testament Studies: Deuteronomy*, 19; Miles, *A God of Many Understandings?*, 59–62.

distinction made between the God of Israel and the gods of other ANE people has less to do with the interpretation of the worshipers and more to do with the nature of the being who is worshipped. The remainder of this section will serve to fortify the conclusions of Miles and Rofé.

The content of Deuteronomy is largely focused upon the Law given to Moses in the Exodus account. Now, if we interpret the *Shema* as teaching true monotheism, as stated above, such a contention is problematic for those scholars who seek to redefine the first commandment of the Decalogue, as recorded in both Exod. 20 and Deut. 5—just a few verses prior to the *Shema*.[12] Some interpreters propose that the first commandment in the Law of Moses is an acknowledgment that other gods exist but that the Hebrews ought to worship *Yahweh* alone.[13] However, given that Deuteronomy functions as a commentary or restatement via application of the Law of Moses, it is untenable to hold to a henotheistic interpretation of Exod 20:3, particularly if it implies a reversal of Deut. 5:7 as well. Oswald Allis makes a similar proposition but expands it beyond the immediate context of Deuteronomy. For Allis, the very fact that the author of Genesis and Exodus refers to the God of Israel as the sole Creator of the universe necessitates a monotheistic interpretation of this commandment.[14] A distinction that seems to naturally flow from the data, then, is that theological propositions differ from religious commands. While the author of the texts in question may be theologically affirming monotheism, he is not ignoring the fact that some Israelites hold to a less-than-monotheistic view of the world around them. So, the content of the religious command should not be seen as a disavowal pertaining to the objective reality of monotheism, but as an acknowledgment of subjective henotheistic practices among the Hebrew people.

Even more damning to the notion that henotheism is represented in the first commandment is John Sailhamer's observation that "other gods" is a reference to dead, wooden idols.[15] He substantiates this claim by noting Deut. 28:36, which states: "The LORD will bring you and your king whom you set over you to a nation that neither you nor your fathers have known. And there you shall serve other gods of wood and stone." The crux of

---

12. Walton, *Zondervan Illustrated Bible Backgrounds Commentary: Volume 1*, 456.

13. Mills and Wilson, *Mercer Commentary on the Bible*, 147; Matthews, *Old Testament Turning Points*, 77.

14. Allis, *God Spake by Moses*, 74.

15. Sailhamer, *The Pentateuch as Narrative*, 285.

Sailhamer's argument, then, is not that the author of the Pentateuch denies that men worship false gods, but that these gods (as represented in idols) are not qualitatively deity. Furthermore, if one is to assume a consistency in authorship and worldview within the Pentateuch, it would mean that the author presumably applies the *Shema* concept of monotheism throughout the text. Therefore, based upon Sailhamer's argument, it appears proper to interpret statements pertaining to deity, within the Pentateuch at-large, through the lens of *Shema* monotheism.

Returning specifically to the *Shema*, John Frame makes the following observation: "God is one being (quantitatively) because there is only one Lord (qualitatively)."[16] This nuanced understanding of qualitative deity is most helpful and will be referenced throughout the course of this chapter. For Frame, just as those authors previously mentioned, the *Shema* must be understood in the greater context of Deuteronomy, in which frequent monotheistic affirmations occur.[17] For instance, in Deut. 4:32–39, the author states twice that there is no other God beside *Yahweh*. In verse 35 the author states, "Know that the LORD is God; there is no other besides him." Again in 4:39 an equivalent statement is made, ". . .The LORD is God in heaven above and on the earth beneath; there is no other." Compare these affirmations to what is stated in Deut. 32:39 when the author writes, ". . .there is no god beside me. . ." Such a series of pronouncements seems to lay the matter to rest. Yet, statements such as these do little to convince Bernard Anderson and Steven Bishop.

These authors believe that references such as those mentioned only make sense in the context of poetic literature that refers to *Yahweh* as superior to other gods.[18] Anderson and Bishop propose that not until the latter portion of Isaiah could one say that Israel takes upon itself explicit monotheism. For Anderson and Bishop, all early monotheistic statements are more in line with expressed allegiance to a national God rather than a belief in only one God.[19] Still, given the material presented thus far, the position taken by Anderson and Bishop does not seem to be the best explanation of the data. For proof of their position, one need only look in one of the books they routinely cite: Deuteronomy.

---

16. Frame, *The Doctrine of God*, 622.

17. Ibid, 622–623.

18. Anderson and Bishop, *Contours of Old Testament Theology*, 64.

19. Ibid, 66.

Taking into account what has been seen thus far in the *Shema* and other texts in Deuteronomy, the data presented makes the most consistent sense by assuming monotheism. This is especially true when one considers that the author of Deuteronomy records an insistence that the worship of other "gods" through sacrifice is actually the worship of demons (Deut. 32:17). Thus, while logically not the only way to interpret the data, the most consistent and plausible interpretation of the information in Deuteronomy is monotheism.

THE BASIS OF THE TRINITY: MONOTHEISM AND HENOTHEISM IN THE OLD TESTAMENT

The issue of monotheism in the Old Testament can be rather complex, depending upon one's approach to this topic. As K.L. Noll observed, the distinctions necessary to differentiate monotheism and henotheism are often subtle.[20] Due to the lofty language utilized by henotheists to speak of their god as opposed to other gods, one could easily misunderstand their verbiage for that of a confused monotheist. Moreover, one could just as easily read the words of committed monotheists and come to the conclusion that they are henotheists.[21] The subtle difference is often that the henotheist acknowledges multiple beings who are, by their very nature, gods. In contrast, the monotheist readily makes reference to and believes in the existence of created spiritual beings entirely different from God, but who could nevertheless be mistaken as gods.

Horst Dietrich Preuss begins addressing the issue of early Israelite religion by discussing the problematic "God of our ancestors" passages.[22] In assessing the patriarchal data regarding Abraham, Isaac, and Jacob, Preuss seems to believe that these three central figures adhere to a common ANE ancestral deity understanding of *Yahweh*. While *Yahweh* was different from all other gods, His distinction was in that He called Abram and became the God of His people.[23] Preuss then perceives progress occurring at the time of Moses in which there is a distinct step forward from Israel being a people who adhere to tribal adoration of deities, to becoming solely dedicated

---

20. Noll, *Canaan and Israel in Antiquity*, 132.

21. Ibid, 132; Bright, *A History of Israel*, 145.

22. Preuss, *Old Testament Theology: Volume II*, 7.

23. Ibid, 8–10.

to *Yahweh*.[24] Still, one can see an amalgamation of theological concepts, according to Preuss, by the usage of *El* designations in conjunction with *Yahweh*.[25]

Walther Eichrodt comes to conclusions similar to those of Preuss. For Eichrodt, it is beyond question that the early Israelites believed in many gods.[26] He argues that the majority of the "early" Old Testament assumes the existence of many gods.[27] In noting this proposed assumption, Eichrodt chides those who use monotheistic theology as the test for the truth of a given religious system. Pressing the issue further, Eichrodt cites numerous passages which he recognizes as teaching that there are many gods in existence, rather than *Yahweh* alone.[28] Walther Zimmerli comes to the same conclusion as Eichrodt. After citing the same or similar passages as Eichrodt, he states, "Yahwism did not simply eliminate the notion of alien deities, however much it considered *Yahweh* alone the only divinity for Israel. Israel knows nothing of any theoretical monotheism."[29]

Even a cursory interaction with the propositions laid forth by Preuss and Eichrodt (and Zimmerli, for that matter) reveals a number of tenuous assumptions and questionable reasoning. First, Preuss predicates his entire argument on the assumption that the Pentateuch is a document comprised of information from many different authors. Although some scholars ardently contend for this position, this contention is debatable at best.[30] Additionally, Preuss sees support for his assumptions in the fact that he believes much of the Old Testament and its theology originated in the seventh century before Christ. Therefore, if the theory that multiple authors with multiple motivations composed the Pentateuch is demonstrated to be false, the arguments presented by Preuss lose their strength.

In the case of Eichrodt, he, too, assumes a very late dating for the composition and content of the Old Testament books and theology. Moreover, many of the passages he uses to support his contention for a belief in many gods fall far short of demonstrating his assertion (most of these are addressed throughout the course of this chapter). Special attention

24. Ibid, 8.

25. Ibid, 8–10.

26. Eichrodt, *Theology of the Old Testament: Volume I*, 220.

27. Ibid, 220–221.

28. Ibid, 220–223.

29. Zimmerli, *Old Testament Theology in Outline*, 42.

30. Archer, *A Survey of Old Testament Introduction*, 89–189.

will be given to the three texts purported to support Eichrodt's position. The first text in which he sees henotheistic tendencies is Judg. 11:23–24. Because Jephthah states that his God gives Him land and Chemosh gives the Moabites their territory, Eichrodt assumes that the text is teaching that there are many gods. Yet, can such an assumption be justified? Would it not be more probable that the author of Judges is merely describing the conversation that occurred, rather than using the narrative to prescribe a belief in many gods? Likewise, it is highly debatable whether Jephthah was affirming the existence of the god Chemosh. Given the Moabite belief in Chemosh, it would not serve Jephthah well to ignore the Moabite belief that a god named Chemosh gave them their territory when Jephthah is arguing that *Yahweh* gave the Hebrews their land. Thus, it could be argued that this text is more of a description of a conversation than a statement of theology.

Eichrodt also cites II King 3:27 as clear evidence that the Israelites believed in territorial gods. Yet, the text itself only states that the king of Moab sacrificed his son as a burnt offering during a battle with the king of Edom. The text then states that a great wrath fell upon the warriors of Israel and so they returned to their land. While on the surface Eichrodt's contention seems to have some validity, his argument loses strength when one considers what the text does *not* say. There is no mention of wrath coming from Chemosh. There is also no mention of gods being engaged in the battle. Further, the deity routinely referenced in the narrative is the God of Israel. So, although there is a burnt offering by the king of Moab and wrath falls upon Israel, the text does not say where the wrath originated, and nowhere does the author imply that the trouble comes from a territorial god.

The last text set apart for consideration by Eichrodt is I Samuel 26:19. The author of this passage records an exchange between David and King Saul. During the course of their dialogue David states that the Lord intends to drive out of Israel the evil men inciting the conflict between himself and Saul, and declaring that they should serve other gods. Again, superficially Eichrodt appears to have a point. However, given the context of the Old Testament texts mentioned thus far in support of Hebrew monotheism, Eichrodt seems to be ignoring the obvious in assuming that this reference is intended to convey henotheism. Unless Eichrodt's seventh century composition theory is correct, the uniform teaching regarding other gods in the early Old Testament (that they are no gods at all) remains true. Therefore, to tell someone they must go serve other gods is to tell them to serve dumb and deaf idols. Further, it needs to be pointed out once again that this text is descriptive of a conversational exchange and that it is not prescriptive regarding the content of theology.

Interestingly enough, critical scholarship has begun to make a shift in approaching the problem of monotheism versus henotheism in the Old Testament. R.W.L. Moberly's essay in *Early Jewish and Christian Monotheism* combines a revealing admission along with critical presuppositions. Moberly states, "First, although the Bible presents a picture that is apparently monotheistic from the outset, monotheism. . .only emerged relatively late in Israel's history during the biblical period. . ."[31] While Moberly's statement implies that monotheism is the initial theological framework of ancient Israel, his assumptions regarding the date of the OldTestament come into play. Moberly can concede that conservative scholarship is correct in asserting that the entire Old Testament is monotheistic, because he believes that much of the content of the Old Testament was either written in the sixth century before Christ or was edited and altered during this same period.[32] So, in avoiding the conclusions of thrse data, Moberly needs only to adhere to his late dating of the Old Testament.

Although not the focus of this research, it should be noted that documentary models and late-dating arguments for the Old Testament are fiercely debated in scholarly circles. Some of the concerns raised against this approach to the Old Testament text are worth mentioning. First, on the part of critical scholars, there is an assumption that the Old Testament is a product of literary development and has little to no divine revelation at its basis.[33] This assumption posits the conclusion that the Old Testament is a purely literary product, prior to the examination of the data. The end result then is that the data must be interpreted through the lens of an already assumed conclusion. Second, due to the assumed conclusion, all references throughout the Old Testament that point toward authorship consistency are easily dismissed as later revisions.[34] Again, in this scenario the conclusion drives the research rather than the research resulting in the conclusion. Third, those holding a naturalistic approach to the Old Testament assume that ancient authors could not nuance their writings in such a way as to write differently based upon audience, stage of life, and intended purpose

31. Moberly, "How Appropriate is 'Monotheism' as a Category for Biblical Interpretation?," 216.

32. Smith, *God in Translation*, 187–215.

33. Archer, *A Survey of Old Testament Introduction*, 113.

34. Ibid, 114.

for writing.[35] Even though modern authors are generally praised for being able to tailor their writings (even within a single volume) to multiple audiences for a variety of purposes, ancient authors are not afforded such ability. Therefore, all changes in grammar, tone, and purpose are assumed to be a result of revision or additions to the text rather than being the product of a skilled author.

Yet the entire issue of dating the book of Deuteronomy (or the entire Old Testament, for that matter) and any potential revision of the Old Testament is a moot point for the LDS adherent. In appealing to LDS authoritative texts, Joseph Smith believed the book of Deuteronomy to have been penned long before any proposed exilic revisions (1 Nephi 5:11; 3 Nephi 20:23). While the dating of the Old Testament and proposed revisions to its text are worth debating, the issue itself is related to, but not directly important for, the data examined within the present research.

While some scholars have demonstrated an evolutionary progression from ANE recognition of a god named *El* to the Israelite acknowledgment of *Elohim* as God, this connection proves little regarding early Israelite monotheism. To the contrary, Bernard Anderson and Steven Bishop have argued that the *El* forms present throughout the Old Testament indicate that the worship of *Yahweh* undertook an evolution of sorts from Canaanite religion into the faith of Israel.[36] As proof of this adoption, Anderson and Bishop cite the interaction between Abraham and Melchizedek.[37] This example is superficially quite persuasive. However, there is an equally and perhaps canonically more viable proposal. If the text of Scripture is to be believed, then one must assume its clear teaching that monotheism preceded polytheism.

One text that could be levied in support of this proposition, outside of the narrative of Adam and Eve, is Gen. 4:26. This passage discusses antediluvian peoples (or pre-historical peoples) calling upon *Yahweh* as God. Still, some see the implication of this passage as being complicated by what *Yahweh* is recorded as telling Moses in Exod. 6:3.[38] According to this passage, *Yahweh* does not reveal Himself to Abraham, Isaac, and Jacob as *Yahweh*, but as *El Shaddai*. Thus, it could be argued that Exod. 6:3 undermines the implications of Gen. 4:26. However, even a superficial reading of each

35. Ibid.

36. Anderson and Bishop, *Contours of Old Testament Theology*, 63.

37. Ibid, 64.

38. Becking, *Only One God?*, 81.

passage contradicts this conclusions. If people prior to the deluge called upon *Yahweh*, in no way does this contradict the fact that *Yahweh* did not reveal Himself as *Yahweh* to Abraham, Isaac, or Jacob. In short, these texts are referring to two different groups at two different times and reveal different aspects of the same being.

Returning specifically to the topic of original monotheism, Winfried Corduan argues for the existence of monotheistic religions among preliterate tribes, he writes:

> Since there is good reason to believe in the common descent of all human beings from the original pair, both on revelatory and scientific grounds, it is logical that the monotheistic religions practiced by preliterate tribes do, in fact, derive from the same monotheistic beliefs and practices attributed to the earliest humans in special revelation.[39]

Therefore, in Corduan's estimation, the Israelite adoption of monotheism is not something new but rather a restoration of the old. Yet, regardless of whether or not the original monotheism theory can be substantiated, one fact remains that is assumed by both Christian and LDS adherents: the first persons were solely devoted in worship to the Creator God. So, while important, the positions being contrasted in this research (Nicene Orthodoxy and LDS tritheism) both assume the viability of revealed texts.

John Walton contends that one significant distinction between *Yahweh* and the gods of the ANE is that, while the ANE gods had origins, the God of Israel was without beginning and distinct from the created order.[40] One aspect of the evolutionary model of religion that Walton sees in the Old Testament is the ANE concept of a divine council.[41] However, the council in the Old Testament differs from that seen elsewhere in the ANE. The Old Testament text implies that, instead of the council being composed of gods, it is made up of created beings.[42] Furthermore, the council is never explicitly acknowledged by Old Testament authors but instead appears to be more of a background concept that has been understood through the lens of monotheism. In Walton's view, the Old Testament does not contain

---

39. Corduan, *A Tapestry of Faiths*, 41–42. For a fuller exposition of Corduan's research into original monotheism see *In the Beginning God*, 2013.

40. Walton, *Ancient Near Eastern Thought in the Old Testament*, 87–91.

41. Ibid, 94.

42. Ibid, 95.; Cf. Korpel, *A Rift in the Clouds: Ugaritic and Hebrew Descriptions of the Divine*, 314.

the common ANE tiered understanding of divine beings consisting of a high god, lesser gods, and intermediate beings. Instead, there is *Yahweh* and the created heavenly beings. Although there are certainly distinguishing nuances that could be explored regarding ANE divine council concepts and those found in the Old Testament, the main argument is simply this: the council concept in the Old Testament is substantially different than the ANE conception. Therefore, the Old Testament council should not be assumed as evidence for the worship of a High God but rather as making sense of the ANE notion of a divine council/assembly in light of Israelite, revelational monotheism.

John Oswalt goes beyond the proposals of Walton by not only stating that the Israelites viewed reality differently than the ANE, but that they were radically different *because of* their monothesitic convictions.[43] While recognizing that some passages within the Old Testament seem to allow for the existence of beings described as gods, Oswalt proposes that they are of an entirely different category than *Yahweh*.[44] In fact, Oswalt classifies the Old Testament approach to other "god" beings as "vehemently and continuously" resolute that *Yahweh* alone is not just Israel's God, but that He alone is qualitatively God.[45] Following this same line of argumentation, Richard Bauckham interprets much of the early Old Testament as not denying the existence of beings worshipped as gods but as denying them being qualitatively deity in the same sense as *Yahweh*.[46] Admittedly, Bauckham does classify this more as monolatry rather than monotheism, but his point still resounds: the early Israelites did not just view *Yahweh* as uniquely their God, but as the unique God who is entirely different from any other lesser divinities.[47]

Todd Miles follows a comparable line of reasoning, believing that, although Scripture recognizes the existence of beings worshipped as gods, they are created beings who are subjectively designated as gods by those worshipping them.[48] Citing numerous Scripture passages[49] that connect the worship of idols with the worship of demons, Miles surmises that all

43. Oswalt, *The Bible Among the Myths*, 23.

44. Ibid, 64.

45. Ibid.

46. Bauckham, *God Crucified*, 15.

47. Ibid.

48. Miles, A God of Many Understandings?, 59–60.

49. Deut. 32:17; Lev. 17:7; Isa. 34:14; Ps. 106:37–38.

instances of affirming "gods" in the Old Testament are nothing more than allusions to the demonic activity behind the idols being venerated.[50] Such an interpretation is consistent with the Apostle Paul's understanding of idols as representations of demons as stated in Gal 4:8 and 1 Cor 10:20.

Beyond what is mentioned in Deuteronomy, the Old Testament is replete with references to there being but one God. In Isa. 44:6–8 and Isa. 45:5–22, the prophet Isaiah frequently declares that there is but one God. In Isa. 44:6–8, the prophet records, "I am the first and I am the last; besides me there is no god. . .Is there a God besides me? There is no Rock; I know not any." This language is consistent with the terminology used in Isaiah 45:5–22:

> I am the LORD, and there is no other, besides me there is no God. . .there is none besides me; I am the LORD, and there is no other. . .I am the LORD, and there is no other. . .And there is no other god besides me, a righteous God and a Savior; there is none besides me. . .For I am God, and there is no other.

In the very next chapter, Isaiah records God as stating that He alone exists as God. As if to make a statement regarding his qualitative nature, Isaiah records *Yahweh* as stating, "there is none like me" (Isa. 46:9). In his commentary on Isaiah, John Oswalt proposes that the repetitive statements that there is no other God does not question the allegiance of some to idols, nor does it imply that there are no spiritual beings acting as gods.[51] Instead, the God of Israel is the only being that could rightly be described as God because of His attributes, nature, and acccomplishments. Therefore, *Yahweh* alone could be qualitatively described as God. To worship any other is to worship a being that is not qualitatively deity, but rather weak and powerless, especially in comparison to the sovereign Lord, *Yahweh*.[52]

Similar statements are made elsewhere in the Old Testament. 2 Sam. 7:22 states, ". . .For there is none like you, and there is no God besides you. . ." Compare this with 1 Kgs. 8:60 which records, "That all the peoples of the earth may know that the LORD is God; there is no other." How should these affirmations of monotheism be understood in relation to passages that speak of other "gods" (i.e. Exod. 15:11; cf. Ps. 82:1)? Should these texts be interpreted as implying that Scripture actually teaches henotheism

50. Ibid, 60–66.

51. Oswalt, *The New International Commentary on the Old Testament: The Book of Isaiah*, 215–227.

52. Wolf, *Interpreting Isaiah*, 197–199.

rather than monotheism? Based upon the following consideration, the answer can only be no.

While Scripture may refer to beings other than *Yahweh* as "gods," it never does so with clarity as to whether they actually exist as deities. Even when mentioned in Scripture, these gods are portrayed as existing in the minds of their worshippers but are never affirmed as actual beings with whom *Yahweh* must contend. An example of such a scenario can be seen in Elijah's exchange with the priests of Baal (1 Kgs. 18). The Apostle Paul also declares that any being masquerading as a god is not by its nature a true god (Gal. 4). The text of Scripture reveals that those worshipping false gods believe them to be real, but this worship is a far cry from the authors of Scripture claiming that other gods actually exist as gods.

Interestingly, in delving deeper into what the Apostle Paul writes regarding this issue, the content of the *Shema* is applied to the issue of polytheism. In 1 Cor. 8:4–6, Paul writes of idols and gods as merely "so-called gods." He then launches into an application of the *Shema* to the issue of idols. For Paul, there are clearly idols or even beings that some call gods, but they are not truly gods. Why not? Because, in Paul's view, the *Shema* passage precludes the possibility that beings who are truly deities exist outside of *Yahweh*. Therefore, rather than being tempted by the numerous opportunities for pagan worship among the polytheistic Corinthians, Paul declares that there is but one being who is truly God and worthy of Christian worship.[53] Likewise, in his book *The New Testament and the People of God*, N.T. Wright has argued that Hebrew monotheism could never be confused with henotheism. In Wright's evaluation, the creational nature of Israel's monotheism rules out the possibility of henotheism precisely because it demands that there be only one creative being. If there is but one creative being, only He could be considered God in an ontological sense.[54]

In the final analysis, to embrace the proposition that the Israelites were henotheists runs counter to Old Testament evidence. Moreover, by accepting a henotheistic framework, one must also concur with the evolutionary theory regarding Israel's monotheism. Even though one may see some evolutionary elements in the Old Testament text within the beliefs of the people, the contention that the foundation of Israelite religion is a move from animism to polytheism and then henotheism is to ascribe to

---

53. Ryken and LeFebvre, *Our Triune God*, 62–63.
54. Wright, *The New Testament and the People of God*, 249.

an anti-supernatural position.[55] It is precisely because the Old Testament proposes that God has revealed monotheism that it should be seen as normative for revelationally-derived Hebrew theology. If the authors of the Old Testament were developing their theology *ad hoc*, it would make more sense for them to insist that the patriarchs discovered monotheism and then had their belief confirmed by *Yahweh*. Instead, *Yahweh* acts and imparts knowledge to Abraham. This scenario stands in distinction to the polytheistic or henotheistic beliefs of the people surrounding Israel.[56] Therefore, the proposal that early Israelite monotheism is actually henotheism is far from an established fact.

THE TRINITY IN THE OLD TESTAMENT

When discussing plurality within unity implied in the Old Testament, much is made of Gen. 1:26, a text utilizing the Hebrew word *Elohim*. This passage, Gen. 1:26, clearly portrays *Elohim* as an example of plural-unity. The passage reads: "Then God said, Let Us make man in Our image, according to Our likeness. . ." The significance of this text is in the fact that God refers to Himself as plural while declaring there is but a single image in which man is to be made.

Some anti-trinitarians could object to this use by noting that Psalm 82:6 translates *Elohim* as "gods." Therefore, *Elohim* should be seen as supporting a plurality of "gods" rather than a single God. It is true that *Elohim* is accurately translated as "gods" in Psalm 82:6; however, when *Elohim* is used as a name for God it is ontologically in the singular sense.[57] Still, it is a matter of undisputed fact that *Elohim* is a plural form; it is the singular *El* with the plural suffix *im*. Allis notes that although *Elohim* is a plural form, it is used in a singular sense throughout the Old Testament when referencing the true God of Israel.[58] Further, given the Old Testament preoccupation with denouncing the pagan polytheism of Gentiles, it makes little sense to understand the usage of *Elohim* as having any hint of a polytheistic conceptual framework. The Hebrew conception of God is entirely unique among

---

55. Harrison, *Introduction to the Old Testament*, 381–395.

56. Johnston, *Religions of the Ancient World*, 29.

57. Geisler, *Systematic Theology, Volume 2*, 277.

58. Allis, *God Spake by Moses*, 9.

the ANE religions and therefore cannot be merely dismissed as a variant form of polytheism or monolatry.[59]

There are others who believe that the "Us" and "Our" statements could not be representative of the Trinity, instead believing that this plural terminology is "plural of majesty" construct.[60] Simply speaking, this means that a person in a position of royalty in an ancient culture would, on occasion, speak of himself in the plural form (e.g., I Macc. 10:19; 11:31). Therefore, Gen. 1:26 should be seen as nothing more than a regal pronouncement. In fact, Old Testament scholar Horst Preuss believes that this reference is most likely an instance of the plural of majesty.[61] A major weakness in Preuss' plural majesty assertion is that there are no examples of an Old Testament king using plural majesty language when referring to himself.[62]

German scholar Claus Westermann believes that there is no evidence for a plural of majesty usage in ancient Hebrew, and therefore interpolating this literary device into the text of the Old Testament should be abandoned.[63] Thus, to merely dismiss the "Us" and "Our" designations as a plural of majesty is to root one's understanding in a concept foreign to ancient Hebrew. This is not to say that plural forms that could be interpreted as majestic plurality do not appear in the Old Testament, because they certainly do (see Ezra 4:18). However, the plural of majesty is a less-than-viable approach to the "Us" and "Our" statements in Genesis 1:26. This approach should be abandoned because royal, and plural majesty have no support among the Hebrew kings, nor are there many parallels to such a concept in the verbs and pronouns making up the Old Testament.[64] The absence of such language, coupled with the plural and singular interchange in the text, cause the plural majesty argument to lose strength.

John Sailhamer contends that Gen. 1:26 is an allusion to the triune nature of God. His conclusion is based upon the fact that God created a plurality of genders in His image, which is but a single image. This reference casts the image of God as a plural unity vaguely analogous to the human male-female relationship in creation.[65] Based upon the data, the

---

59. Walton, *Ancient Near Eastern Thought in the Old Testament*, 110.

60. Theissen, *Lectures in Systematic Theology*, 90.

61. Pruess, *Old Testament Theology: Volume I*, 147.

62. Grudem, Systematic Theology, 227.

63. Westermann, *Genesis 1–11: A Commentary*, 145.

64. Clines, *On the Way to the Postmodern*, 460.

65. Sailhamer, *The Pentateuch as Narrative*, 95–96; Cf. Vanhoozer, *First Theology*, 67.

historic Nicene interpretation of Gen 1:26 is that *Elohim* is not a plurality of gods, but a reference to a single God: a single God who is plurality within unity. This is made apparent by the fact that a plurality of persons (male and female) coming together as one flesh is the ultimate expression of the image of *Elohim*. An example of unity is located in Genesis 2:24, when Adam and Eve are described as becoming "one (*'echad*) flesh." One should note that, while they become "one," Adam and Eve do not lose their distinctive personhood.

Elsewhere in the Old Testament, triadic repetitions regarding the name of the Lord seem to have a Trinitarian connection. In Numbers 6:24–26, the author writes "The LORD bless you and keep you; the LORD make his face to shine upon you and be gracious to you; the LORD lift up his countenance upon you and give you peace." The mention of the LORD in triplicate leads John Frame to see a connection between this passage and the apostolic benediction contained in II Corinthians 13:14.[66] Given the Apostle Paul's repeated use of such benedictions, Frame's application is quite plausible. Similarly, twice in the book of Isaiah a triadic designation is given to the name or person of God. In Isaiah 6:3, God is called "holy" three times. In Isaiah 33:2, the prophet uses the name LORD three times, along with three different descriptions of the LORD as judge, lawgiver, and king. Although these references do not prove the doctrine of the Trinity nor demonstrate it clearly, the use of terms and various designations in triplicate does lend credence to the Nicene reading of these Old Testament texts.

It is also significant that a multiplicity of divine persons are mentioned in various Old Testament passages. The use of "He" (the Father) and "His Holy Spirit" in Isaiah 63:9–10 could be interpreted as allusions to the first and third persons of the Godhead. John Frame connects the Isaiah passage to what he believes to be an explicitly Trinitarian passage, Haggai 2:5–7. For Frame, it would seem that the reference to "My Spirit" is to the Holy Spirit, "the LORD" is the Father, and "the treasures of all nations" is a reference to God the Son as the Messiah.[67] While not overly technical in his approach to the references given, Frame stands in line with historic Nicene hermeneutical approaches to these texts.

In light of this material, it is interesting that the possibility of plurality existing in a monotheistic Godhead is an active topic in pre-Christian Jewish theology. A text that inspires much of this debate is found within

66. Frame, *The Doctrine of God*, 635.

67. Ibid, 637.

Daniel's book of prophecy. In Daniel 7:9, a plurality of thrones exists in heaven, all of which, the text proposes, belong to *Yahweh*. Daniel writes, "I kept looking until the thrones were set up, and the Ancient of Days took His seat. . ." In the passage there are multiple seats of power (thrones), yet a single being of power (the king). N.T. Wright, commenting on pre-Christian Judaism, points out that, "Within the most fiercely monotheistic of Jewish circles. . .there is no suggestion that 'monotheism' or praying the *Shema*, had anything to do with the numerical analysis of the inner being of Israel's God Himself."[68] Wright's assertion may be true, but it must be admitted that it makes little sense for the *Shema* to function as an analysis of *Yahweh's* inner being. While it has been argued that the Old Testament uniformly teaches monotheism, there are certainly no didactic passages providing theological details as to the nature of *Yahweh* in His essence. Given that the Old Testament narratives also address issues pertinent to their intended audience, it would be less than productive to provide an exposition regarding *Yahweh's* nature. Why? To state it simply, the Israelites struggled greatly with breaking away from the polytheism of their neighbors; holding fast to conceptual monotheism was difficult enough, let alone Trinitarian monotheism. The latter monotheism only arises in the New Testament after Second Temple Judaism had firmly established monotheism as its theological foundation. This foundation was built upon after direct experience with the Messiah provided the avenue by which to understand the nature of *Yahweh* experientially prior to formulating theological, Trinitarian conceptions.

In summary, allusions to unity within plurality clearly exist within the Old Testament. While not stated as explicitly as in the New Testament or resulting creeds, the prospect of a pre-Christian Trinitarian theology is presented by terminology and grammar utilized throughout the Old Testament. From the perspective of historic Nicene orthodoxy, the most natural reading of the Old Testament is in fact a Trinitarian reading.[69]

HEBREW MONOTHEISM AT THE BIRTH OF CHRISTIANITY

Given the background of Old Testament monotheism presented thus far, it would be beneficial to investigate the major monotheistic themes present in Israelite theology at the time of Jesus' life and ministry. Certainly, the Old

68. Wright, *The New Testament and the People of God*, 259.
69. Warfield, *The Works of Benjamin Breckinridge Warfield: Volume II*, 141–142.

Testament Scripture constitutes the scriptural background for the monotheism undergirding Trinitarianism. However, it is pertinent to the direction of this research to establish, in broad terms, the general understanding
of monotheism just prior to the beginnings of Christianity.

From the time of the exodus event until the birth of Christ, the Israelites experienced numerous socio-political changes. Further, from the sixth-
century B.C. forward, the Hebrew people had fallen under the captivity
or rule of foreign peoples. The exposure of the Israelites to pagan cultures
and religious systems instilled in the Israelites a greater level of disdain for
idolatry and polytheistic religious systems.[70] Although this may not have
been the normative, folk-level result for all Israelites, these monotheistic
sentiments held true on a national level. Additionally, interaction with Hel-
lenism led to an approach among the Israelites to not just view *Yahweh* as
uniquely God, but as wholly other, even to the point of avoiding speaking
His name.[71] Moreover, as Larry Hurtado has observed, Israelite religion in
the intertestamental period took on a staunchly exclusive flavor.[72] Considering the manner in which many Israelites adopted the social practices of
pagans and Hellenists, it is quite noteworthy that their religious convictions
grew all the more. Even though the level to which early Israelites adhered
to monotheism at the folk-level is debated, the monotheistic practices of
the Roman era are rather pronounced and undeniable.[73] What comes next
will be a recounting of the scriptural witness as to how this understanding
of monotheism was shaped by the experiential interaction with *Yahweh's*
tri-personal revelation in the history.

THE PERSONS OF THE TRINITY

The monotheistic background of the Old Testament and Second Temple
Judaism was stretched or expanded based upon the experience of early
Christians with three distinct persons who are all referred to as deity. The
persons seen throughout the text of Scripture are revealed as Father, Son,
and Holy Spirit. Passages pertinent to establishing the deity of the three
divine persons revealed through the Scriptures will now be examined. The

70. Scott, *Jewish Backgrounds of the New Testament*, 267–268; Nuesner, *Judaism When Christianity Began*, 3.

71. Scott, *Jewish Backgrounds of the New Testament*, 268–269.

72. Hurtado, *Lord Jesus Christ*, 30.

73. Ibid, 29.

course taken follows that of the presentation in creedal Trinitarian theology. Namely, that the first person of the Trinity is the Father, the second person is the Son, and the third person is the Spirit. Therefore, the deity of each person will be examined in the aforementioned order.

The Persons of the Trinity: The Father is God

Throughout Scripture, the Father is acknowledged as full deity. In the Old Testament the Fatherhood of God is established very early in the Pentateuch. In Exod. 4:22–23, Israel is referred to as God's child. While not explicitly calling Himself "Father," the implication of this quality is undeniable. In Deut. 8:5 and 14:2, the fatherhood of God is again implied by a reference to the Israelites as His children. This is similar to the implication in Isa. 1:1–2. God is explicitly referred to as Father for the first time in Deut. 32:6b. As a lyric in the Song of Moses, the author writes, "Is not he your father, who created you, who made you and established you?" The remainder of the chapter contains multiple references to God as Father (Deut. 32:8–9, 18–20). Throughout the Psalms, the Psalmist refers to God as Father. He is called the "Father of the fatherless. . ." (Ps. 68:5), David's Father (Ps. 89:26), and a Father who pities His children (Ps. 103:13). The prophet Isaiah also calls God "our Father" multiple times (Isa. 63:16; 64:8).

While the Old Testament contains at least twenty references to God as Father, the New Testament designation of God as Father increases exponentially and with great levels of specificity. Most of the New Testament references to God as Father are seen in His relationship to God the Son, Jesus.[74] In fact, all but three New Testament letters make reference to God as Father in direct relationship to Jesus as God the Son.[75] The manner in which the relationship of the Son to the Father elucidates the personhood of God the Father can be seen by the number of times God is called Father in the gospel accounts. In John's Gospel alone, God the Father is mentioned 137 times. Admittedly, this designation is found mostly in the discourses occurring within the narrative and mostly from the mouth of Jesus.[76] Further in the Synoptics, God is called Father 138 times.[77] Thus, in the gospels accounts alone, the deity of God the Father is affirmed a total of 275 times.

74. Cooper, *Our Father in Heaven*, 109.

75. Coppedge, *The God Who is Triune* ,24.

76. Köstenberger, *A Theology of John's Gospel and Letters, 370–371.*

77. Morris, *New Testament Theology*, 248.

John Cooper speaks to the New Testament concept of Father by stating, "Thus, the God of Scripture is not merely the universal *Father*, an idea found in other religions. He is the Father of Jesus Christ, the Son. This is what distinguishes the New Testament faith from all other religions."[78] Cooper also believes that it is this robust Father-to-Son relationship revealed fully in the New Testament that provides grounding for recognizing an undeniable distinction in the persons of the Godhead.[79] It would seem then that the transition from the use of Father as a generic epithet of God in the Old Testament, to the specificity among divine persons in the New, is critical for understanding the biblical doctrine of the Trinity.

The New Testament references to God the Father are numerous in the Pauline writings and the Gospels. For instance, in Rom. 1:7 Paul greets the church at Rome by referencing the grace and peace of God the Father and the Lord Jesus. Notably, Paul makes a distinction between the Son and the Father, yet recognizes the deity of both by the manner in which he links the two persons. Likewise, in his letter to the Galatians, he writes of being an Apostle of Jesus sent by God the Father (Gal. 1:1). Paul once again links Jesus and the Father in such a way as to make clear their distinctiveness but to imply their qualitative sameness.

In the Gospel of John, Jesus calls God, "the Father" (John 6:27). Again, in John 6:46, Jesus identifies the Father as God, while also proclaiming His own deity, stating: "Not that anyone has seen the Father, except the One who is from God; He has seen the Father." In John 20:17, Jesus tells Mary that He is ascending to the Father who is God. In the Synoptics (Matt. 6:9; Mark 14:36; Luke 1:21) Jesus prays to the Father and refers to Him as *Abba*. This Aramaic term denotes a personal, Father-to-Son relationship. Such a personal, intimate prayer to God as Father is utterly unique among the Hebrews of Jesus' day.[80] Interestingly, the Apostle Paul goes on to explain that those in Christ can call on God by also addressing Him as *Abba* (Rom. 8:15; Gal. 4:6). Even as Jesus is dying on the cross He speaks to God as Father, commending His spirit into the hands of the Father (Luke 23:34,46). However, regardless of the New Testament emphasis upon God the Father as the Father of God the Son, there is still a consistent New Covenant theme regarding the Fatherhood of God to all believers. Jesus even emphasizes this point when in Matt. 6:9. He begins His model of prayer for the disciples

---

78. Cooper, *Our Father in Heaven*, 109.

79. Ibid.

80. Jeremias, *The Prayers of Jesus*, 57.

by referring to God as "Our Father."[81] Undoubtedly, the Fatherhood of God is assumed throughout Scripture.

The Persons of the Trinity: The Son is God

Though Jesus never says, "I am God," He does use other language which inescapably leads to the conclusion that Christ acknowledges that He is God in the flesh. This is important because it is the coming of the Son in the flesh that reveals the triune nature of God. Thus, more attention will be directed to establishing the deity of the Son than either the deity of the Father or the Spirit. The rationale for this is as follows: First, the deity of the Father is assumed within the text of Scripture. Second, the deity of the Spirit is directly connected to the deity of the Son. The manner in which the Spirit's ministry is connected to that of the incarnate Son produces something of a "domino effect." If the Son is God, then, based upon the sending of the Spirit from the Father and the Son, the Spirit is God. To state it another way, Thomas Forsyth Torrance writes, ". . .The central focus of the Gospel upon the Deity of Christ is the door that opens the way to the understanding of God's triune self-revelation as Father, Son, and Holy Spirit."[82] Therefore, what follows is an interaction with pertinent passages establishing the deity of Jesus Christ.

The Persons of the Trinity: The Son as God in John's Gospel

The Prologue to the Gospel of John immediately asserts the deity of Jesus. In John 1:1–3, John writes, "In the beginning was the Word, and the Word was with God, and the Word was God. He was in the beginning with God. All things were made through him, and without him was not any thing made that was made." In John 1:1, God (*theos*) by definition is understood to be deity. However, John goes further and stretches the bounds of monotheistic theology by referring to the Word as *theos*. For John, it is a matter of importance to begin his narrative by applying an affirmation of deity to the incarnate Son. According to John 1:14, the "Word" referenced is the incarnate Son, Jesus Christ. John's assertion that the Word becomes flesh

---

81. Lightner, *The God of the Bible*, 145.
82. Torrance, *The Christian Doctrine of God*, 49.

and dwells among the people calls to mind the idea of the tabernacle in the Old Testament.[83] Therefore, Jesus is God "tabernacling" among His people.

Returning to John 1:1–3, John is arguing that God the Son existed before the created order and was with God (*pros ton theon*). John begins his account of the life of Jesus by establishing the distinction between Christ and the created order. Moreover, John equates the nature of the Word (the Son) with God (the Father). Thus, John sets out to establish the deity of Christ from the first line of his account.[84]

In the fifth chapter of John's account, Jesus makes a series of claims that place Him on the same level as the Father. John 5:18 reads, "For this reason therefore, the Jews were seeking all the more to kill Him, because not only was He breaking the Sabbath, but He was calling God His own Father, making Himself equal with God." While some have argued that this text does not imply total equality in every respect, it still brings forth the idea of qualitative or essential equality with God the Father.[85] In the same passage, Jesus raises people from the dead and claims to be the giver of life (John 5:21), an attribute the Old Testament attributes solely to God (Deut. 32:39; 1 Sam. 2:6; Ezek. 37:12–14).

Christ claims to share the glory of the Father in John 17:5. He says, "Now, Father, glorify me together with Yourself, with the glory which I had with You before the world was." Jesus is referencing Isa. 42:8: "I am the LORD, that is My name; I will not give My glory to another. . ." If *Yahweh* does not share His glory, and Christ claims to share *Yahweh*'s glory, then Jesus is equating Himself with the Father.

The Persons of the Trinity: The Son as God in the Synoptics

During His trial, Christ is asked, "Are You the Christ, the Son of the Blessed One?" Jesus responds by saying, "I am; and you shall see the Son of Man sitting at the right hand of Power, and coming with the clouds of heaven" (Mark 14:61–62). In short, Jesus claims to be the promised Messiah. According to the prophet Isaiah, the Messiah would be God. Isaiah writes that, "His name will be called Wonderful counselor, Mighty God (*el' gibbor*), Eternal Father, Prince of Peace" (Isa. 9:6). Some scholars allege that Isaiah

---

83. Blomberg, *The Historical Reliability of John's Gospel*, 74; Bowman and Komoszewski, *Putting Jesus in His Place*, 138–139.

84. Thielman, *Theology of the New Testament*, 154.

85. Blomberg, *The Historical Reliability of John's Gospel*, 110–112.

was teaching that the Messiah would be a god-like hero, not God in the flesh. While the word *el'* in a plural form can refer to a mortal man, Isaiah only uses this word as a designation for God.[86] In the context of the passage, the reader is supplied with a contrast between the Messiah's humanity as a child (*yeled*) and His deity as the heroic God (*'el gibbor*), the Messiah of His people.[87] Therefore, based upon the context, this Being is not a god-like hero but is in actuality the hero-God.

Additionally, in Christ's response at His trial, He calls Himself "The Son of Man." This title refers to an Old Testament prophecy found in Daniel regarding the coming Messiah. Daniel 7:13–14 reads:

> Behold, with the clouds of heaven One like a Son of Man was coming, and He came up to the Ancient of Days and was presented before Him. And to Him was given dominion, Glory and a kingdom that all the peoples, nations and men of every language might serve Him, His dominion is an everlasting dominion which will not pass away; and His kingdom is one which will not be destroyed.

The designation Ancient of Days is previously used in Dan. 7:9–13 for God the Father. Thus, according to the prophet Daniel, the Messiah (Son of Man) is distinct from the Ancient of Days, yet fully shares his deity and attributes.

In Matt. 8:23–27 Jesus is recorded as calming a storm by merely speaking to it. Elsewhere, Jesus exercises His power over nature and the sea by walking on water (Matt. 14:25; Mark 6:48; cf. John. 6:19). Yet, the Old Testament states that it is God alone who has power over the sea (Ps. 107:23–32; cf. Isa. 43:16). In fact, in the book of Job, it is said of God: "Who [God] alone stretched out the heavens and trampled the waves of the sea" (Job 9:8). What is revealed then is that Jesus possesses power over nature that God alone holds. Therefore, the picture painted in the Synoptics is one of the Messiah, Jesus, sharing in the attributes and actions of *Yahweh*.

The Persons of the Trinity: The Son as God in the Apostolic Witness

Outside of the gospel accounts, the New Testament contains numerous references to, and declarations of, the deity of Christ. In Col. 1:15, Jesus is described as the visible manifestation of God. The passage begins by referring

---

86. Young, *The Book of Isaiah: Volume III*, 336.

87. Ibid, 337.

to Christ as, ". . .The image of the invisible God. . ." (*eikōn tou theou tou aoratou*). Linguistically, the text is calling the reader to understand Christ as the exact likeness of the invisible God. Based upon the scriptural teaching that the Father cannot be seen and is in fact a Spirit (John 1:18; 4:12), this likeness then does not refer to physical form but rather to His divine nature.

Perhaps the most explicit reference that demonstrates the deity of Christ outside of the Gospel accounts is in Phil. 2:6–11. Paul begins by describing the crux of the Trinitarian doctrine: the incarnation. He says of Christ, "Who, though he was in the form of God, did not count equality with God a thing to be grasped" (Phil. 2:6). When Paul writes that Jesus was in the "form" (*morphē*) of God, he is making an assertion regarding the nature of Christ. Georg Strecker believes that this statement is meant to convey that Jesus is *essentially* equal to God the Father.[88] Yet, Strecker's belief that Paul is stressing essential equality appears to be contrary to the plain meaning of *morphē*. Commenting on this passage, Moises Silva writes, "If we stress the classical usage of this term, the technical sense of Aristotelian philosophy suggests itself: *morphē*, although not equivalent to *ousia* (being, essence), speaks of characteristic attributes. . .."[89] In confirmation of Silva's analysis, Verbrugge comments on Paul's usage of *morphē* stating ". . .that the essential nature of Christ is defined as a divine nature, which is thought of as existing 'in' divine substance and power."[90] It is reasonable then to interpret "form" as a sphere of existence based upon the nature of Jesus' being.[91] Further, Jesus does not use His equality with God the Father as something to be exploited (*harpagmos*) or used to His advantage.[92] It would seem that Strecker's cautious position of "essential equality" is too weak, given the strength and weight of Paul's language.

Paul's use of this passage in reference to Jesus is significant because of the text to which it refers, Isa. 45:18–25. This text is one of the strongest affirmations of monotheism and the uniqueness of *Yahweh* found within the entire Old Testament. Paul's intention here is clear; rather than a transgression of Old Testament monotheism, the recognition of Christ as God

---

88. Strecker, *Theology of the New Testament*, 72.

89. Silva, *Philippians: BECNT*, 100.

90. Verbrugge, *New International Dictionary of New Testament Theology*, 377.

91. O'Brien, *The New International Greek Testament Commentary: Philippians*, 210–214.

92. Oakes, *Philippians*, 193.

is a fulfillment of Hebrew monotheism.[93] Such an application to Christ is astounding because, as E.J. Young has noted, Isa. 45:18–21 indicates that there is but one God and He alone is the Creator.[94] So, in Paul's theology, Christ is not just a god but the very God who is the only God. Given the fact that even those adhering to evolutionary understandings of Old Testament monotheism recognize Isa. 45:18–25 as a distinctively monotheistic statement, Phil. 2:6–11 is an application of monotheism to the recognition of Jesus Christ as deity. From the Nicene perspective, the only manner by which to understand this application consistently is through creedal Trinitarianism.

The Persons of the Trinity: The Son of God as the Son of the Father?

Some older English translations of the Bible utilize the most unhelpful formulation "only begotten." The phrase translated in the King James Version as "only begotten Son" is *monogenēs huios*. However, contrary to LDS contentions,[95] one should not take this in a literal, physically paternal sense. For instance, *huios* (son) has been used metaphorically throughout the New Testament. In Mark 3:17, James and John are referred to as "Sons (*huios*) of Thunder." Furthermore, in Gal. 3:26 Paul writes that all believers are "Sons (*huios*) of God." These references are clearly intended to be figurative. The translation of *monogenēs* as "only begotten" is a result of the King James translators retaining Jerome's Latin translation of the term *ūnigenitus*, meaning, "only begotten." However, the Latin text existing prior to Jerome's translation does not use the Latin *ūnigenitus* when describing God the Son; instead, it utilizes the term *ūnicus*, meaning "only."[96]

In order for the Greek manuscript to warrant the translation "only begotten," the Greek term being translated would need to be *monogennetos*. To translate *monogenēs* as "only begotten" is less than precise. Commenting on this mistranslation, James White notes that:

> The key element to remember in deriving the meaning of *monogenēs* is this: it is a compound term, combining monos,

93. Carson and Beale, *Commentary on the New Testament Use of the Old Testament*, 837–838.

94. Young, *The Book of Isaiah: Volume III*, 210–215.

95. McConkie, *Mormon Doctrine*, 546–547.

96. Moody, "God's Only Son: The Translation of John 3:16 in the Revised Standard Version," 214.

meaning only, with a second term. Often it is assumed that the second term is *gennasthai/gennao*, to give birth, to beget. But note that this family of terms has two nu's, *vv*, rather than a single nu, *v*, found in *monogenēs*. This indicates that the second term is not *gennasthai* but *gignesthai/ ginomai*, and the noun form, *genos*.[97]

The term *genos* means "kind," or "race."[98] When the two terms *monos* and *genos* are combined, the reference is intended to convey that Christ is unique and the only one of His kind.[99] Frank Thielman makes a similar argument when he states that, ". . .*monogenēs* means 'one of a kind,' rather than *ūnigenitus* (Vulgate) or 'only begotten' (KJV)."[100] Additionally, William Mounce explains that *monogenēs* can only be understood as stressing the unique nature of Christ; it cannot and should not be understood to imply any type of biological siring.[101]

This metaphorical understanding of sonship is demonstrated in the book of Hebrews. The author of Hebrews (11:17) refers to Isaac as Abraham's "only begotten son." Making use of the same term found in John 3:16 to describe the Father-to-Son relationship (*monogenēs*), the author of Hebrews notes the unique nature of Isaac as the promised child from God. The LDS reader will readily admit that Abraham had multiple children; therefore, the intent of the text is to stress that Isaac is Abraham's unique son, not his only son.[102]

Craig Keener believes the use of the term *monogenēs* in John 3:16 is intended to call to mind the traditional Hebrew understanding of Isaac.[103] Just as Abraham gives Isaac, God the Father has not given merely a son but the unique, beloved Son with whom there is no comparison. Given the fact that it is through Isaac's bloodline that Jesus, as the Christ, has come, Keener's application of *monogenēs* makes sense of the consistent teaching of both the Old and New Testaments regarding the Messiah's relationship to Abraham's son.

97. White, *The King James Only Controversy*, 201–202.

98. Carson, *Exegetical Fallacies*, 30.

99. Rogers and Rogers, *The New Linguistic and Exegetical Key to the Greek New Testament*, 185.

100. Thielman, *Theology of the New Testament*, 154.

101. Mounce, *Mounce's Complete Expository dictionary of Old Testament and New Testament Words*, 1214.

102. Carson, *Exegetical Fallacies*, 31.

103. Keener, *The IVP Bible Background Commentary: New Testament*, 270–271.

In the same manner, Christ should be understood as the unique, one-of-a-kind, "Son of God." Christ's Hebrew contemporaries understood His claim to be the Son of God as an equation with God rather than a statement of biological origin. The Gospel of John records (John 19:7) that when Jesus stands before Pilate, the Jewish authorities charge, "We have a law, and by that law He ought to die because He made Himself out to be the Son of God." Thus, His sonship should be understood as implying deity, not a biological origination.

The text of Scripture further demonstrates that the LDS notion of the New Testament portraying Christ as the biological Son of God is something foreign to historic Christian doctrine. The birth narrative in Luke's Gospel makes no mention of a natural conception resulting from a sexual union. After Gabriel informs Mary that she will carry a son, she asks how this can be, because she has yet to be with a man (Luke 1:34). Gabriel replies, "The Holy Spirit will come upon you, and the power of the Most High will overshadow you; and for that reason the holy Child shall be called the Son of God" (Luke 1:3; cf. Matt. 1:18–24). The narrative is completely devoid of any sexual interaction between God the Father and Mary; rather, the reader is informed that it is through the working of the Holy Spirit that the virgin conceives. What is more, all three persons of the Trinity are mentioned with the Father, being referred to as "the Most High." Thus, the text of both John's and Luke's Gospels depict Christ as uniquely, rather than biologically, the Son of God. Further, Christ is the Son of God not because of conception, but because of His economic relationship to the Father.

The Persons of the Trinity: The Spirit is God

The biblical text not only accords full deity to the Father and Christ, but to the Holy Spirit as well. In fact, the scriptural assertion that God is Spirit nearly makes the deity of the Holy Spirit an underlying assumption. Yet, because of the distinctions made between the persons of the Trinity, the deity of the Holy Spirit cannot merely be assumed to be equal to the Father and the Son. Therefore, it is vitally important to note instances in which the Holy Spirit is recognized as deity in the same sense as the Father and the Son. For instance, in Matt. 28:19, the role of the Spirit in baptism is identical with that of the Father and Son. In Mark 3:28–29, Jesus speaks of those who blaspheme the Holy Spirit. Yet, throughout the text of Scripture, blasphemy is a sin committed against God alone.[104]

In Acts 5:3–4, Peter equates Ananias' lie to the Holy Spirit as being a lie to God. While Ananias certainly lies to the community of faith, the issue according to Peter is that Ananias attempts to deceive God by lying to the Holy Spirit. In Rom. 15:30, all three persons of the Trinity are represented as equals. Paul appeals to the Christians in Rome by the power of Jesus Christ and the Spirit in the love of God. Thus, Paul's appeal assumes a triunity among the persons of the Godhead. 1 Cor. 2:10–11 depicts the Spirit as having the same omniscience as God the Father. Paul states that the Spirit searches all things, including God, and that there is nothing hidden from Him, including thoughts. This attribute of God is also seen in the Old Testament writings of the Psalmist. The Psalms declare that the Spirit shares the omniscience, as well as the omnipresence, of God the Father (Ps. 139). The Spirit is said to know all things and to be in all places.

In the book of Jeremiah, God declares the coming of a New Covenant. The author of Hebrews then applies this text to the Holy Spirit in Heb. 10:15–17. Elsewhere, in Heb. 3:7–11, the author states that the words spoken by God in Ps. 95:7–11 are spoken by the Spirit. This presentation naturally leads one to believe that the author of this letter understands the words spoken to the prophet Jeremiah as being spoken by the Holy Spirit.

Throughout the text of the New Testament, the close relationship of the Spirit to the Father and the Son is discussed in passing or is assumed in various narratives. As John Walvoord observed, the Holy Spirit is often associated with the Father and the Son in a manner that implies His deity. Notice the chart below which represents a summary of relationship passages (cf. Walvoord, 1991:10).

104. Frame, *The Doctrine of God*, 686.

Relational Association	Description and Reference
The Father	1. Spirit of God (Gen. 1:2; Rom. 8:9);
	2. The Spirit of the Lord (Luke 4:18);
	3. The Spirit of our God (I Cor. 6:11);
	4. His Spirit (Num. 11:29);
	5. The Spirit of Jehovah (Judg. 3:10);
	6. Your Spirit (Ps.139:7);
	7. Spirit of the Lord God (Isa.61:1);
	8. Spirit of your Father (Matt.10:20);
	9. Spirit of the Living God (2 Cor. 3:3);
	10. My Spirit (Gen. 6:3);
	11. Spirit of Him (Rom. 8:11);
	12. The Spirit of Truth from the Father (John 14:17; 15:26).
The Son	1. The Spirit of Christ (Rom. 8:9);
	2. Spirit of Jesus Christ (Phil. 1:19);
	3. Spirit of Jesus (Acts 16:7);
	4. Spirit of His Son (Gal. 4:6);
	5. The Spirit of the Lord (Acts 5:9).

Table 1: The Holy Spirit in Relationship to the Father and the Son

The way in which the New Testament authors attribute the Spirit's relationship to both the Father and the Son speaks volumes towards an understanding the deity of the Holy Spirit.

In John Calvin's estimation, passages such as Isaiah 48:16 demonstrate that the Holy Spirit shares in the sovereign control of the Father in sending forth the prophets. Further, in looking into the New Testament, Calvin sees the significance of Paul's teaching that God will choose for Himself a temple because of the Spirit's indwelling presence. Calvin writes, "Now it ought not to be slightly overlooked, that all the promises which God makes of choosing us to himself as a temple, receive their only fulfillment by his Spirit dwelling in us."[105] For Calvin, the deity of the Spirit is undeniable precisely because of His actions as God among the people of God.

---

105. Calvin, *Institutes of Christian Religion*, 76.

In the final analysis, in terms of scriptural presentation, the Holy Spirit is afforded identical divine attributes and activities as the Father and the Son. Still, it must be admitted that the deity of the Holy Spirit is not referenced as often as either the Father (whose deity is assumed throughout Scripture) or the Son. Nevertheless, as James White points out, this understated approach to the deity of the Spirit is not due to any inferiority, but precisely because the role of the Spirit is to point men to Christ.[106] In the economy of salvation, the Spirit's work is less explicit but still demonstrates His deity. As a result, He should be acknowledged as full deity.

The Trinity in the New Testament

Throughout the New Testament the three persons of the Trinity are mentioned together. At the baptism of Jesus (Matt. 3:16–17), the Father, Son, and Spirit are all described as being present and distinct from one another. Also in Matthew's Gospel, in the Great Commission passage, disciples are commanded to baptize converts in the name of the Father, Son, and Spirit (Matt. 28:19). What this text illustrates, as D.A. Carson has observed, is that the missionary endeavors of the Christian faith have always been Trinitarian in nature.[107] Commenting on this very issue of Gospel proclamation, Fred Sanders writes ". . .the gospel is Trinitarian, and the Trinity is the gospel. Christian salvation comes from the Trinity, happens through the Trinity, and brings us home to the Trinity."[108] For Sanders, from the Great Commission forward, the entire New Testament witness to the gospel is Trinitarian. But is Sanders overstating the Trinitarian nature of the gospel message of salvation? In briefly examining two specific references, Sanders' assertion is affirmed. For instance, in Eph. 1:4–13, the Apostle Paul speaks of the Father predestining believers in Jesus (the Son) for salvation, which is sealed by the indwelling of the Holy Spirit. In Titus 3:4–6 God the Father is referred to as "our Savior" who has saved believers by His mercy, having renewed them by the Holy Spirit who was poured out through Jesus Christ. At the very least, in these two references, which speak explicitly of salvation, Sanders seems to be accurate in his proposal.

Outside of the gospel accounts, the apostles refer to the Godhead in triadic form. In 1 Cor. 12:4–6, the variety of spiritual gifts are contrasted

---

106. White, *The Forgotten Trinity*, 139–140.

107. Carson, *The Expositor's Bible Commentary: Volume 8*, 598.

108. Sanders, *The Deep Things of God*, 10.

with the plural unity of the Spirit, Lord, and God. 2 Cor. 13:14 contains a similar reference in which Paul uses a familiar benediction mentioning the grace of Jesus Christ, the love of God, and the fellowship or unity of the Holy Spirit (cf. Eph 2:8). In his letter to the church at Ephesus, Paul speaks of one Spirit, one Lord, and one God (Eph. 4:4–6). Other apostles mention the three persons in their letters. In 1 Pet. 1:1–2, the apostle Peter greets his readers by noting that it is God the Father who has elected them and the Holy Spirit who has sanctified them because of Jesus' shed blood. Jude, the half-brother of Jesus writes of praying in the Holy Spirit, remaining in the love of God, and looking toward the mercy of Jesus Christ (Jude 20–21). In John 15:26 the promise of the Spirit's coming includes the Son speaking about the Father and the Spirit as distinct persons. Jesus says "But when the Helper comes, whom I will send to you from the Father, the Spirit of truth, who proceeds from the Father, he will bear witness about me." Elsewhere Paul uses an equivalent formula in mentioning the coming of the Holy Spirit. Paul writes that this is so because the Father has sent the Spirit of the Son so that believers can cry out "Abba! Father" (Gal. 4:6).

Returning to the Trinitarian nature of the missionary endeavor given in the Great Commission, the New Testament declaration that salvation is provided for sinners is rooted in Trinitarian theology. In the book of Hebrews, the author twice connects salvation to the triune God. In Heb. 9:14 the author writes, "How much more will the blood of Christ, who through the eternal Spirit offered himself without blemish to God, purify our conscience from dead works to serve the living God" (cf. Heb. 10:12–18; 29–31; Eph. 1:3). Thus, the very center of enscripturated revelation, the redemption of sinners in Christ, is grounded in the triune nature of God.

Allan Coppedge has argued that the New Testament data that references the persons of the Trinity is compelling when one understands its frequency. He has demonstrated that numerous passages identify at least two persons of the Godhead, and in some cases, all three. The following represents a reworking and adaption of his findings in chart form.[109]

---

109. Coppedge, *The God Who is Triune*, 34–35.

Two Persons Mentioned	Three Persons Mentioned
1. Matt. 1:20–23; 28:19	1. Mark. 1:10–11; 16:19
2. Luke 1:35; 24:49	2. 1 Cor. 2:1–4; 15:57
3. John. 1:32–34; 20:21–22	3. 1 Pet. 1:2; 5:10
4. Acts 1:3–5, 7–8; 28:23, 25	4. Jude 20–21
5. Rom 1:1–4, 7; 15:30	5. Gal 1:3; 6:7–8, 16–17
6. 1 Cor. 1:3,	6. Eph 1:3; 6:23
7. 2 Cor. 1:2, 21–22; 13:14	7. Phil. 1:2; 4:19–20
8. 1 Thess. 1:3–5; 5:18–19	8. Col. 1:2; 4:12
9. Gal. 1:3	9. 2 Thess. 1:2; 3:5
10. Phil. 1:2	10. 1 Tim. 1:2; 6:14
11. Jas. 1:1	11. 2 Tim. 1:2; 4:1
12. Rev. 1:4–6; 22:17–18	12. Titus 1:4
	13. Heb. 1:1–2; 13:20
	14. 1 John 1:3; 5:20;
	15. 2 John 3,9
	16. Phlm. 1,3
	17. Jas. 1:1
	18. 2 Pet 1:2

Table 2: Passages that mention the Persons of the Trinity Together

When considered as a whole, the abundance of references to the multiplicity of persons in the Godhead is quite compelling.

The entirety of the New Testament abounds with references to three distinct persons: Father, Son, and Spirit, who are all God. As one reads the content of the New Testament in particular, it would almost appear to assume that a Trinitarian hermeneutic will be applied to its content. John Frame believes that the manner in which the doctrine of the Trinity is woven within the fabric of Scripture (i.e. the doctrine's truthfulness is assumed and not explicitly stated) demonstrates that it is not an item of doctrinal debate.[110] The New Testament information presented in this chapter does provide some support for Frame's contention. However, given the creedal evolution that occurs in the early church immediately following the era of

110. Frame, *The Doctrine of God*, 639.

the apostles, it seems that Frame may be overstating his case. B.B Warfield, on the other hand, follows the early Christians' argument that enscripturated revelation was entirely Trinitarian.[111] Yet, it is going too far to state that the doctrine of the Trinity as an explicit article of faith was settled and established during the lives of the apostles. That is to say, the Trinitarian assumption was made implicitly during this period, even if it was not yet stated explicitly. Creedal Trinitarianism was still growing. This topic will be discussed in the next chapter.

CONCLUSION

At the beginning of this chapter, we stated that this section of research is necessary to answer one of the secondary research questions germane to the overall purpose of this project. That question, "what is the systematic teaching of Scripture regarding the doctrine of the Trinity," has been addressed and answered in the following manner. First, it was demonstrated that the early biblical data regarding the worship of *Yahweh* was monotheistic rather than henotheistic. Certainly, the Israelites frequently departed from true monotheism; however, the revealed text of Scripture prescribes monotheism. This portion of research is critical to establishing the theoretical basis for the doctrine of the Trinity, monotheism. Second, the staunchly monotheistic context of Second Temple Judaism was presented as the backdrop for the birth of Christian theology. It was after the advent of Christ that the dynamic nature of God became evident. It was because of this direct contact with Deity that Christians became experiential Trinitarians. How one reconciles the experience of God's self-manifestation in a plurality of Persons with the affirmation of monotheism is what leads to creedal Trinitarian theology (discussed in chapter 3). Third, through the course of this chapter, it was demonstrated that the text of Scripture repeatedly affords full recognition of deity to each of the persons of the Trinity. It is the unified assertion of the Old Testament authors that there is but one being who is qualitatively God. It is the unified teaching of the New Testament that the Father is God, the Son is God, and the Spirit is God, but there is only one God. As John Calvin cautions, Christians must not understand the biblical language regarding persons and their names as denoting division, but distinction only.[112] This is the very issue the early

111. Warfield, *The Works of Benjamin Breckinridge Warfield: Volume II*, 143.

112. Calvin, *Institutes of Christian Religion*, 78.

church wrestled with in understanding the nature of God. The Scripture demonstrates that the Father and Son are distinct persons who love one another (John 3:35; 5:20; 14:31; 15:9; 17:23–26) and speak to one another (John 11:41–42; 12:28; 17:1–26). Further, the Holy Spirit is a person, like the Father and Son, who can think and speak of His own accord (John 16:13; Acts 1:16; 5:3; 8:29; 10:19; 11:12; 15:28; Rom. 8:26). Additionally, the Holy Spirit is a distinct person who is distinguishable from both the Father and the Son (Luke 3:22; Rom. 8:27–34). Yet, how does one accommodate, in creedal form, the plurality of persons revealed in Scripture with the affirmation of monotheism?

The data presented in this chapter answers the research question posited; however, it does not reveal how the early church codified their experiences with the scriptural witness into creedal, Nicene orthodoxy. Thus, what must come next is a thorough tracing of Trinitarian creedal development founded upon the witness of the Old and New Testaments throughout the life of the early church. We will interact with important theological works in the early church leading up to the time of Augustine (A.D. 354-430). We can now move beyond the basis of Nicene orthodoxy, the Scriptures, to the historical development of Nicene Trinitarianism.

Chapter 3

The Development of Nicene Orthodoxy

INTRODUCTION

The previous chapter sought to establish the basis for Nicene orthodoxy rooted in the exegesis of enscripturated revelation. This chapter will endeavor to answer the following research questions: First, what is the historical, orthodox position on the Trinity and how early was it established? Second, how is the doctrine of the Trinity currently being addressed among orthodox theologians? These questions will be answered by interacting with important theological works in the early church leading up to the time of Augustine (A.D. 354–430). Any Trinitarian exploration must begin with Scripture, followed by an assessment encompassing the historical developments pertaining to the Trinity.

This logic is based upon two observations: First, contemporary theology has been directly influenced and grounded by the theological development and struggles of the early church. In short, the theology of the early church directly influences the theology of today. All contemporary, theological dialogue takes place in light of a long history of theological struggle. To ignore this fact is to assume that theology occurs within a historical and cultural vacuum, which it does not. Theology develops and contours itself in response to the questions being asked during a given time period. This theological struggle and reshaping is true even of contemporary theology.

Every few decades a new or revived theological trend pushes orthodoxy further in definition and application. In short, this theological fine-tuning is an organic process that will and should continue with each new generation of theologians. Second, the issues that dominated the Patristic period matter because, whether consciously acknowledged or not, the way Christians read Scripture has been influenced by formulas and decisions birthed in the early church.

The scriptural case for a belief in three persons, yet only one God, has already been presented. Therefore, it should be abundantly clear to the reader that the doctrine of the Trinity is not an attempt to transcend the bounds of the Scriptures' straightforward teaching, but to echo it in creedal form. The development of creedal Trinitarianism is a result of the early church seeking to make sense of two distinct questions. First, given that Jesus was God incarnate, what must the nature of God be like? Second, if Jesus was God incarnate, how can monotheists make sense of the Father and the Son both being divine?[1] It is precisely because of the incarnation and direct contact with the divine being that the early church had to reconceptualize their understanding of God's nature. In a sense, members of the early church became experiential Trinitarians, and it is that experience with the incarnate Jesus that acted as the driving force for the resultant creeds.[2]

Moreover, the doctrine of the Trinity does not originate within the bounds of the fourth century. The New Testament church always afforded the triune God His due worship. Because the tripersonal nature of God is found throughout the entirety of the New Testament, it could never be said that the early church (post-New Testament) ever lacked impetus to understand God as triune in some sense.[3] In addition, although the vocabulary used to describe the Trinity required some time to develop, this extended time frame does not seem to be born from an absence of Trinitarian conviction. Rather, the early church lacked a conceptual basis upon which to give full disclosure concerning the triune God's functional hierarchy.[4] The early church faced a linguistic disadvantage when expressing the Trinity to the world around her. For instance, explaining the unity of God without

1. McGrath, *Understanding Doctrine*, 169–170; Allison, *Historical Theology*, 231.

2. Coppedge, *The God Who is Triune*, 13; Pelikan, *The Emergence of the Catholic Tradition (100–600)*, 226.

3. Horrell, "The Eternal Son of God in the Social Trinity," 45.

4. Ibid, 46.

discounting the plurality of persons became problematic. For those with a Stoic background, such as Tertullian, explaining the unity of God as resulting in the persons being *una substantia* (one substance) was deemed too crudely materialistic.[5] Much of the issue in using substance to describe that which anchors the unity of persons while giving rise to the plurality of persons, is in the fact that substance conveyed the idea of "matter."[6] A similar designation for the unity of God was that of "essence" or the divine nature. Even though this terminology was preferred by some in the early church, and even among theologians[7] today, by the time of Nicaea substance and essence became largely interchangeable terms. Still, it must be admitted that linguistically, the definitional barrier between these terms remained strong between the Latin and Greek speaking churches. Given the difficulty within the church in defining terms and agreeing upon adequate designations for what God is in His being, it became all the more troublesome to explain these concepts to a pagan world. Regardless of this difficulty in language, the church needed descriptions and defenses of biblical doctrine in order to survive.[8]

A progressive development of Trinitarian doctrine based upon questions being asked of the church occurred during the first few centuries of history. This doctrinal evolution was a result of increasingly complex answers to questions the church faced concerning the triune God. The inquiries posed to the church resulted from the influences of Gnosticism, Platonism, and Neo-Platonism. What becomes apparent is that while the basis for theology—revealed Scripture— does not change, the complexity and clarity of doctrines change as the community of faith systematizes what is demonstrated within the revealed text.

THE CONTEXT OF THE EARLY CHURCH

In an overview of the early church fathers, it seems that the issues of specific doctrinal formulations are not related solely to the authority or reliability of enscripturated revelation, but also to the proper hermeneutical approach to the text of Scripture.[9] All issues pertaining to heresy and orthodoxy

---

5. Kelly, *Early Christian Doctrines*, 113–114.

6. Ibid, 114.

7. Horton, *The Christian Faith*, 280–281.

8. Soskice, "Biblical Trinitarianism," 128.

9. Fairbairn, *Life in the Trinity*, 1–2.

centered not on contemporary issues of narrative accuracy, but rather on the issue of how to understand the descriptive narrative details in distinction to prescriptive theological statements.[10]

This is not to say that the early church was entirely free from speculation regarding the content of the eventual canonical text. There were certainly books (Antilegomena) whose inspiration was debated in some circles. Additionally, not all of the early church fathers from whom there are extant writings had direct access to all of the New Testament. As Lee Martin McDonald has observed, the data available would lead one to assume that by the close of the second century, most churches had general access to the canonical Gospels and Paul's Epistles, but not the entirety of the New Testament corpus.[11]

In the previous chapter, the New Testament data pertinent to Nicene Trinitarianism focused upon these two generally accepted segments of Scripture (the Gospels and Pauline writings). Therefore, this present chapter will not center upon canonical debates or secondary doctrinal issues concerning which there is much scholarly disagreement. Rather, without ignoring interpretive nuances among the early church fathers, this chapter will intend to examine the development of Nicene Trinitarian thought through the time of Augustine of Hippo. The rationale for focusing upon the time period described is due to Trinitarianism finding a rather settled explanation in the writings of Augustine. Certainly, Trinitarian theology has undergone changes through the centuries following the life of Augustine, but the core content of Augustine's theology has flavored Trinitarian thought for the past sixteen centuries.

We must establish a framework in which to understand the development of the doctrine of the Trinity. As will be demonstrated, the early church fathers were uniformly committed to monotheism and to the belief that the Father, Son, and Spirit are distinct persons, but yet one God. Creedally, this acknowledgment took some time to develop. As with most theological matters, there were attempts to explain the nature of God that did not align with what was revealed in the text of Scripture. These approaches have historically been referred to as heresies. As Alister McGrath has argued, heresy is not generally intended to be destructive, but is always meant to be subversive. Heresy is an attempt to answer theological questions outside

10. Vanhoozer, *Dictionary for Theological Interpretation of the Bible*, 566–570; McKim, *Dictionary of Major Biblical Interpreters*, 1–13.

11. McDonald, *The Biblical Canon*, 298.

the framework of previously accepted theological concepts.[12] Given what will be discussed in the life of Arius later in this chapter, McGrath's contention would appear to be correct. When those who became prolific leaders in sub-orthodox or unorthodox movements taught ideas about God that contradicted the text of Scripture, Christian theologians pushed the clarity of orthodox doctrine further. In short, the development of heresy presses orthodoxy to greater levels of creedal clarity.

During the developmental period of Trinitarian doctrine, the danger of tritheism (as exemplified in Joseph Smith's teaching) was rarely seen, due to the strong emphasis upon monotheism in the early church. However, throughout the course of doctrinal development, the first few hundred years of church history were littered with heresies that emphasized the oneness of God to the detriment of the distinction among the divine persons (as typified by adoptionism and modalism). The most potent or successful of these unorthodox systems was known as Arianism. As will be discussed later, Arianism pushed the already developed Trinitarian dogma to a new level of coherence at the Council of Nicaea.

A second factor in the progressive development of Trinitarianism must been seen in the state-sanctioned persecution. The pagan theological attacks from the Roman state led many Christian writers to explain the Christian understanding of God in detail when defending the beliefs of the church to government officials. Further, due to the violent nature of the persecution, Christian adherents needed increasingly to understand what doctrines were worth dying for. Nevertheless, persecution also served to hinder, in many ways, theological development. Even though the core content of orthodoxy was gaining clarity, the details of orthodox doctrine remained somewhat muddled. In the midst of persecution, Christians were more concerned with understanding and holding to monotheism and a belief in three persons than being able to describe in detail how such beliefs can be consistent.[13] In summary, both heresy and persecution served to further doctrinal perspicuity, while at the same time hampering deep theological exploration.

---

12. McGrath, Heresy, 33.

13. Gonzalez, *The Story of Christianity: Volume I*, 31–57; Frend, *The Early Church*, 35–45, 69–82; Cairns, *Christianity Through the Centuries*, 86–94; Latourette, *A History of Christianity: Volume I*, 81–89.

THE APOSTOLIC FATHERS

The impetus to examine the scriptural representation of the triune God, and to express this mystery in creedal form, did not arise for nearly a century after the completion of the New Testament. Admittedly, no explicit Trinitarian doctrine was offered by the Apostolic Fathers; however, the triadic schema is still implicit in their writings.[14] For example, in his first letter, Clement (c. 45–99) writes of there being only one God. He states further that there is but one Christ and one Spirit (I Clem. 46:6).[15] This triadic schema appears again in the same letter with the phrase, "For, as God lives, and as the Lord Jesus Christ and the Holy Ghost live. . ." (I Clem. 58). Throughout the text of I Clement, the author references the Father as deity (19:2; 35:1–3), the Son as deity (16:2; 59:2), and the Holy Spirit (22:1; 45:2). While not an explicitly Trinitarian letter, I Clement is littered with triadic language.[16]

A similar formulation appears again in the works of Ignatius (c. 50–117). In his Letter to the Magnesians, Ignatius encourages his readers to unity by invoking a triadic schema stating that his readers should prosper in the Father, the Son, and the Spirit (Mag., 13). The formula appears again in his Letter to the Ephesians. In section thirteen, Ignatius addresses the issue of false doctrine, and praises those in Ephesus for resisting false teachers. Ignatius utilizes the triadic concept by likening the Father to stones upon which a building is built; Christ, through the cross, is the instrument of building, and the Holy Spirit is the rope by which believers ascend the building unto God, through faith. Throughout the remainder of the letter, Christ is addressed as God, and prayer to Him is assumed.[17] Although not explicitly described, the Apostolic Fathers recognized, at least in the redemption of mankind, the triune nature of God.

It must be pointed out that first-century letters were not penned to provide a codified theological statement of faith; rather, they were written to address contemporary concerns.[18] Therefore, attempting to find a fully-orbed and systematized theology in the late first and early second centuries would be a futile exercise. The reason for this scenario is that the question

---

14. Rusch, *The Trinitarian Controversy*, 3.

15. Clement, *I Clement*, 46:6.

16. Olson and Hall, *The Trinity*, 17.

17. Rusch, *The Trinitarian Controversy*, 3.

18. Ibid,

of Trinitarian ontology and relational action was rarely, if ever, expressly asked or answered. Therefore, the apostolic writings did not substantially advance Trinitarian theology; instead, they served to synthesize some of the evidence presented in Scripture. As J.N.D. Kelly has noted, this does not mean that they were unequivocally Trinitarian; however, recognition of God's plurality in persons and unity in being is apparent throughout their writings.[19]

THE APOLOGISTS

With the dawn of the second century came the rise of the Apologists, and a new era in Trinitarian discourse. In assessing how early Trinitarian theology developed, the age of the Apologists is of prime importance. The needs of the period demanded further exploration into the nature of God. Confronted by a pagan society, charges of atheism, and the challenge of Greek philosophy, the Apologists sought to explain the nature, function and interaction of the Godhead. They attempted to do so in part in order to distinguish the God of the Christians from pagan gods. Specifically, the Apologists made the first attempt to provide a detailed explanation of the relationship between the Father and the Son in distinction to the pagan concept of divine beings.[20] The Holy Spirit's relationship to both the Father and the Son received less attention in these writings due in large part to the fact that few thinkers outside of the church challenged Christian theology as it related to pneumatology. Instead, the issue of prime importance was the relationship and distinctions between the Father and the Son. Therefore, the data provided by the Apologists reveal that by the early to middle of the second century, a robust Trinitarianism was beginning to take formal shape. This information serves to answer the primary research questions of this chapter by demonstrating identifiable nascent Trinitarianism very early following the close of the New Testament text.

The single greatest contribution to the Trinitarian conversation by the Apologists was the designation of Christ as the *logos*. Utilizing the apostle John's concept, the Apologists capitalized on a notion already pervading in the philosophy of the day. Craig Blomberg explains that *logos* is the concept through which many ancients understood the communication of God (or

---

19. Kelly, *Early Christian Doctrines*, 95.

20. McGrath, *Understanding Doctrine*, 172.

gods for that matter) to human beings.[21] In a very general sense, ancient people understood *logos* to refer to spoken forms of communication, but not words in general. Instead, *logos* was the content or meaning conveyed via the spoken words.[22] However, John's meaning appears to transcend this term's functional usage; instead it touches on the ideas of current and past philosophical discussions. In the pre-Christian apocryphal text, Wisdom of Solomon (7:21–22, 25–29; 9:1–2, 9; 18:4–6), wisdom is endowed with attributes unique to God. There is a personification in which the mind of God takes on attributes unique to a person. This phenomenon is exemplified in the Jewish targums, specifically the Targum Onqelos. In this targum, the memra (Aramaic equivalent of *logos*) represents a direct expression of God's mind, and it is often used in place of God's name (Targum Onqelos to Exod. 4:12). John has taken these pre-Christian ideas and infused them with not just the notion of personification, but actual personhood. It is John's contention that the *logos* is not just the mind of God in some abstract sense, but that *logos* is actually God Himself.[23] Thus, John has taken what was at one time viewed as merely personified attributes of God and actually applied it to a distinct person, Jesus of Nazareth.[24] This linking of Christian to pre-Christian concepts establishes John's understanding of Jesus as having a role in both creation and divine communication to mankind.[25] Further, John's use of *logos* rather explicitly designates Jesus of Nazareth as co-eternal with Yahweh.[26] Therefore, the *logos* epitomizes the manner in which Christ is to be equated with God as a co-eternal, divine person.

Justin Martyr

Justin Martyr (A.D. 100–165) is the apologist who most frequently utilizes the *logos* concept. As Jaroslav Pelikan has argued, Justin possibly adopts this language due to both his philosophical background and a desire to have Christian doctrine taken seriously by thinking peoples.[27] It is im-

21. Blomberg, *Jesus and the Gospels*, 162.

22. Tenney, *The Expositor's Bible Commentary: Volume 9*, 28.

23. Bock, *Jesus According to Scripture*, 410–411.

24. Blomberg, *Jesus and the Gospels*, 210–213; Bock, *Jesus According to Scripture*, 412; Morris, *NICNT: The Gospel According to John*, 104.

25. Bock, *Jesus According to Scripture*, 412–413.

26. Schreiner, *New Testament Theology*, 258.

27. Pelikan, *The Emergence of the Catholic Tradition (100–600)*, 188–189.

possible to definitively interpret Justin's motivations, yet Pelikan's theory is consistent with what is known of Justin and his theology. For instance, Justin believes that Greek philosophy is rooted in the works and theology of Moses (I Apol., 59). Therefore, Justin has no issue with connecting Greek philosophy with the content of Scripture. Such an observation sheds light on why Justin is comfortable with using the *logos* concept to explain the eternal Jesus.

In examining how Justin explains his *logos*-Christology, it is important to note that according to Justin, the *logos* is not just the first-begotten of God, He is God (I Apol., 63). Additionally, in his Dialogue with Trypho, Justin declares that the *logos* is, in fact, God. As Justin explains, the *logos* is one with God the Father but remains distinct in the same manner that a ray of light is distinct from the sun (Dial., 61). For Justin, the rationale behind a multiplicity of divine persons seems elementary. Because the Father conversed before creation with another divine person, there must be a multiplicity of eternal, divine persons while there is but one God (Dial., 61).

Perhaps Justin's view is best represented by the following analogies. Justin understands fire as analogous to the Father-Son relationship. He states that when one flame brings forth another flame by ignition, the first flame is not decreased in its nature as a true flame. Rather, the second flame is distinct and independent but its existence is grounded in the first flame (Dial., 61). As J.N.D. Kelly has argued, for Justin, this distinction in number does not mean that there is a division of essence.[28] Thus, the word is in a sense distinct yet inseparable from the being speaking the word. Within Justin's theology, the "birth" of the *logos* represents a distribution of God but not a severing of the divine nature.[29] Yet, it would seem that for Justin there was a tendency toward subordination. Even though this may not have meant that Justin viewed the Son and Spirit as lesser deities in a qualitative sense, he did see them as economically subordinate to the Father.

Athenagoras

Another noteworthy work, *A Plea for the Christians*, was written by Athenagoras of Athens (A.D. 133–190) to defend the church against the charge of atheism. The significance of this letter is that it was sent to Emperor Marcus Aurelius Antoninus. Therefore, it represents a formal defense of

28. Kelly, *Early Christian Doctrines*, 96–98.
29. Ibid.

Christian theism directed toward the pagan Roman state. In this text, Athenagoras states quite emphatically that the early Christians were not atheists because they were monotheists; that is to say that they acknowledge one divine being, God. Further, Athenagoras states that Christians recognize and worship the Son of God, Jesus. Nonetheless, Athenagoras is careful to point out that the Son of God spoken of by the early Christians should not be understood in the same manner as pagans define "sons" of gods. Instead, the Son of God is the *logos* of the Father, eternal and uncreated, because the Son and the Father are one (Plea., 10).

Not only did Athenagoras dispute the charge of atheism, but he also thoroughly undermined the claim that Christians believe Christ to be the biological Son of God. In writing to a pagan emperor, Athenagoras used highly developed Trinitarian language that avoided the pitfalls of subordinationism to plead his case.[30] At the same time as he pleaded for Christianity, Athenagoras provided an argument for monotheism that appears directed toward dualism (Plea., 8). For Athenagoras, the absolute unity of the divine persons is necessitated by the fact that it is the person of the Spirit who maintains absolute unity.[31] This stands, in Leslie Barnard's view, as the distinguishing factor that prevents Athenagoras from slipping into a form of modalism.[32] Because a plurality of persons is seen as intrinsic to unity, the absolute unity of the Godhead does not diminish the plurality of persons.

Irenaeus

For some Christian apologists within this period, including Irenaeus of Lyon (A.D. 115–199), salvation depended upon the distinction among divine persons. Within Irenaeus' theological system, the Father literally extrapolates the Son and Spirit from within Himself. According to Irenaeus, man's redemption is founded upon the triunity of God. Irenaeus would argue that salvation comes from the Father, through the Son, and is by the Holy Spirit.[33] As a result, salvation is impossible without the work of the triune God. In Irenaeus' estimation, the content of Scripture revealed the

30. Richardson, *Early Christian Fathers*, 296; Barnard, *Théologie Historique: Athenagoras*, 182.

31. Barnard, *Théologie Historique: Athenagoras*, 110.

32. Ibid, 111.

33. Irenaeus, *The Demonstration of the Apostolic Preaching*, 7.

triune nature of God progressively as necessitated in accomplishing the divine plan for salvation.[34]

The nuanced nature of Irenaeus' approach to the Godhead could lead some critics to see him as theologically inclined to Justin's subordinationist tendencies. However, this conclusion is incorrect.[35] Irenaeus tended to borrow heavily from Justin's thought and theology due to his admiration for Justin's intellectual contributions to Christianity. This borrowing, in part, is what has led some to classify Irenaeus as a subordinationist.[36] However, as Denis Minns has argued, the thrust of Irenaeus' theology was not meant to speak directly to the issue of subordination.[37] Instead, Irenaeus focused the majority of his theological musings and writings on the problem of heresy.

The largest emphasis of Irenaeus' works was on the role of the Son in revealing the Father. Because Irenaeus stressed the notion that when one looks upon the Son one sees the full deity of the Father, there is little ground upon which to categorize Irenaeus as a decidedly subordinationist theologian.[38] Instead, it is most accurate to classify Irenaeus as seeing the Son and the Spirit as the "hands of the Father"[39] rather than lesser beings.[40] This analogy represents a distinction to the analogy of the spoken word used by Justin. For Irenaeus, the image of the spoken word is less appropriate.[41]

Irenaeus proposes that there is a clear distinction among the persons of God, but this distinction does not necessitate there being three individual deities (Haer., 2.1.2). In short, Irenaeus assumes that there are economic distinctions between the persons of the Godhead, but not in terms of essence or nature. While there may be a plurality of divine persons, there is not, nor could there logically be, any God but the God of Christianity.

Additionally, Irenaeus was one of the first Christian thinkers to speak explicitly of the Godhead as being one in nature or essence (*Dem.*, 2010:47). As some have observed, if anything, Irenaeus stresses the unity of the Godhead with such ferocity that one could almost mistake him for a

---

34. Lohse, *A Short History of Christian Doctrine*, 44; Torrance, *The Christian Doctrine of God*, 75.

35. Minns, *Irenaeus: An Introduction*, 67.

36. Ibid, 59–60.

37. Ibid, 60.

38. Ibid, 61.

39. Osborn, *Irenaeus of Lyons*, 91–92.

40. Minns, *Irenaeus: An Introduction*, 49; Shelton, "Irenaeus," 43.

41. Rusch, *The Trinitarian Controversy*, 7.

modalist.[42] However, explicit statements on the part of Irenaeus that contradict a modalistic framework are found throughout Irenaeus' writings. One instance worth noting occurs in Against Heresies. In the process of arguing that Jesus is not a lesser being than the Father, Irenaeus contends that the Son was co-eternal with the Father, as a distinct person, prior to the incarnation (Haer., 3.18.1). Such a line of argumentation is not consistent with modalism. While Irenaeus was certainly not a modalist, he insisted that Christians are monotheists.[43] Yet, this monotheistic emphasis did not diminish his belief in three divine persons. In summary, Irenaeus provides a clear and cogent second-century Trinitarian description of God. Even though his Trinitarianism is not overtly developed, it is without question, nascent Trinitarianism.

The Apologists: Summary

In summation, the Apologists strove to explain God's plurality within unity through the conception of the *logos*. They endeavored to do so while at the same time maintaining a distinction between the Father and *logos* that does not divide the divine essence.[44] Furthermore, they attempted to use imagery that stressed the eternal generation of the Son, rather than any language implying origination. The works of the Apologists provide a necessary element in establishing how early Nicene orthodoxy began to take shape. Given the content of their writings, the extant works from the Apologists demonstrate that informal Trinitarian assumptions pervaded their theology. As fruitful as this century of discourse was, an entire formula of Trinitarian orthodoxy would not be adopted as the rule of faith until the fourth and fifth centuries.

42. Lohse, *A Short History of Christian Doctrine*, 44; Kelly, *Early Christian Doctrines*, 86.

43. Shelton, "Irenaeus," 43; Pelikan, *The Emergence of the Catholic Tradition (100–600)*, 177.

44. Rusch, *The Trinitarian Controversy*, 7.

EARLY THEOLOGIANS

Origen

One of the most prolific writers in the early church was Origen of Alexandria (A.D. c. 184–254). A devoted Platonist and allegorical interpreter of the Scriptures, Origen possessed one of the keenest theological minds in the early church.[45] In his theological framework, Origen strives to explain the appearance of three divine persons with the term hypostases (Joh., 1989:2.6). While believing that the three hypostases or persons eternally sprang forth from the same fountain of deity,[46] Origen nevertheless acknowledges both their distinctions and unity.[47]

Michael Haykin asserts that Origen saw the need to express a distinction between the Father and Son, but held firmly to their absolute unity because Origen believed the deity of the Son was dependent upon divine unity.[48] It appears that Haykin's summary is accurate; given the fact that just such a proposition is explored in Origen's Dialogue with Heraclides (1–4). It is Origen's contention that there is not just an economic relationship among the persons of the Trinity, but also a genuine ontology as expressed in his designation of the three persons as *homoousios*. Even though this ontology does not suggest separation, it does necessitate a distinction among the persons of the Trinity. This distinction, however, is not indicative of any order based upon existence. That is to say, there is not a progression of persons in terms of coming into existence within Origen's theology. For Origen, the Son and Spirit are co-eternal.[49] Although not as clearly expressed as his understanding regarding the deity and unity of the Father and Son, Origen provides a rejection of any notion that the Spirit had a time-space origination (Princ., 1.3). What does seem to be at least an underlying concept in Origen's theology is that there is some form of subordination among the persons of the Trinity. Specifically, it would appear that the Son and Spirit, for Origen, are subordinate to the Father.[50]

Moreover, Origen's concept of the Holy Spirit is somewhat confused. While on the one hand declaring the Spirit to be uncreated and eternal,

45. Liftin, "Origen," 123.

46. Lohse, *A Short History of Christian Doctrine*, 46.

47. Lyman, "Origen," 120.

48. Haykin, *Rediscovering the Church Fathers*, 71.

49. Pelikan, *The Emergence of the Catholic Tradition (100–600)*, 191.

50. Fairbairn, *Life in the Trinity*, 45.

Origen also appears to insinuate elsewhere that he is a "creature" of the Son (Joh., 2.10). However, as Michael Haykin has noted, such a confusion was not uncommon due to linguistic shortcomings. It is Haykin's contention that prior to the formal explanation provided by the Council of Nicaea, writers rarely made necessary delineation between *agenētos* (uncreated) and *genētos* (uncreated).[51] Therefore it is better to understand Origen's theology in light of his explicit statements regarding the Godhead rather than the unclear statements. Such an approach takes into account definite statements of triune eternality found in Origen's Commentary on Romans (6.7). Yet, it could be argued that Origen maintains categorical confusion throughout his theological writings regarding the distinction between the *logos* as incarnate being and the *logos* as identified with the second person of the Trinity. What this means for Origen is that he can at once declare that the Son as *logos* is eternal and the *logos* as incarnate had a beginning. In assessing Origen's contribution to Trinitarian development, it becomes apparent that Origen thought deeply regarding the Trinity but rarely wrote or spoke definitively regarding God's Trinitarian nature.

Tertullian

Perhaps the most prolific Ante-Nicene Trinitarian developments resulted from the works of Tertullian (A.D. c. 160–225). He is the first person to use the Latin word *trinitas* in describing the Godhead. The development of his terminology comes as a result of his attempt to defend the personhood (persona) of the Trinity's members without dividing their essential substance (*substantia*) (see especially Apol., 21). For Tertullian, the oneness of God is rooted in His simple, unified nature or substance and not a coming together of separate beings.[52]

Tertullian explains that the triunity of God springs forth from the Father because of His economic role and greatness as the Father. This does not mean that the Son and Spirit are not equally great, but merely that in the theology of Tertullian they are economically submissive to the Father in action and role.[53] While they are functionally distinct, the divine nature is wholly shared so that there is but one divine being or substance.[54]

51. Haykin, *Rediscovering the Church Fathers*, 73–74.

52. Osborn, *Tertullian: First Theologian of the West*, 117; Dunn, Tertullian, 35–36.

53. Osborn, *Tertullian: First Theologian of the West*, 130–131.

54. Ibid, 131.

In his work *Against Praxeas*, Tertullian explains his use and understanding of the language he implements in describing God's triunity. Tertullian asserts that the Father, Son, and Spirit are inseparable from one another. Tertullian goes on to explain that the Father, Son, and Spirit are unified as one being (by implication). Yet, Tertullian emphasizes that this unity or oneness does not diminish their distinction, because each person is genuinely distinct from one another (Prax., 2).

In writing *Against Praxeas*, it was Tertullian's goal to combat the heresy of patripassianism. In order to demonstrate that this form of modalism was false, Tertullian uses a series of images from nature. In Tertullian's estimation, one must understand the Son as coming forth from the Father but not separate from Him. Tertullian likens this to a root pushing forth a tree, a spring giving rise to a river, and the sun which gives off rays of light (Prax., 8). It is Tertullian's position that the differentiation within the Godhead is not qualitative as it relates to deity but is rather distinctive in terms of role or aspects of deity.[55] This type of language provides a foundation for contemporary Trinitarian discourse.

Attempting to speak with formal language when describing the triune God, Tertullian borrows heavily from the popular argot of his era's legal system.[56] Despite his linguistic contributions to Trinitarian theology, Tertullian's terminology was not warmly received by the church at large for two reasons. First, his concepts are largely material in nature. An example of this material conception is Tertullian's description of the Trinity in Latin, *tres personae, una substantia*. The Greek-speaking church initially questioned the orthodoxy of such a statement. In the centuries following Tertullian's writings, it became evident that his theology was not heretical, but rather that the language barriers between Greek and Latin inhibited lines of theological communication. Second, his eventual conversion to Montanism caused many to look upon him as a heretic. Regardless of these issues, his language in describing the triune God set the stage for what would be discussed at Nicaea.

THE COUNCIL OF NICAEA

Throughout the second and third centuries, the works of the Apologists served to engage both the church and her critics in dialogue by explaining

55. Lohse, *A Short History of Christian Doctrine*, 45.

56. Latourette, *A History of Christianity: Volume I*, 145.

the nature of the Christian God. Despite the accomplishments of previous centuries, the fourth century brought with it seeds of controversy. Lewis Ayers proposes that the following question was the impetus for the fourth century Trinitarian controversy: How should one understand the distinction between the Father and the Son?[57] The answer to this query introduced a standard for orthodoxy, which has remained virtually unchanged to this day. Although the preceding centuries furthered Trinitarian theology, it is the codified statement that comes from Nicaea that provides much of the theological center for this research. The information examined thus far demonstrates that Trinitarian elements were present in the writings of the early church. Yet, for nearly two millennia it has been Nicaea that has stood as the lens by which to assess orthodoxy. Therefore, in order to adequately evaluate the tritheism of Joseph Smith, the issues that gave occasion to the Council of Nicaea must be explored. In the midst of the turbulence in which the church found itself at the start of the fourth century, one controversy emerged as more potent than the rest. Sparked by the works of an Alexandrian presbyter named Arius (A.D. 250–336), the issue that took center stage became known as the Arian controversy. According to Arius, Christ was not unbegotten; that is to say, there was [a time] when He did not exist.[58] Arius argues that the Son is not eternal but had an origin. Therefore, He is different from the Father not just in person but also in nature, because unlike the Father, the Son was created.[59] Arius believed that the doctrine of eternal generation would render God divisible and composite. Thus, Arius envisioned the God of the Scriptures not as progressively revealed to be Father, Son, and Spirit but as progressively becoming as much due to the creation of the Son.[60]

The goal in Arius' writings is not to challenge orthodoxy, but rather to uphold it in the face of teachings he believed were tantamount to polytheism. As Bernard Lohse has argued, for Arius, the developing Trinitarian creedalism was diminishing the transcendence of the Godhead.[61] After a series of letters and a number of local Egyptian councils, the church was left with no choice but to confront Arius at Nicaea. The council, convening from

57. Ayers, *Nicaea and its Legacy*, 3.

58. Hanson, *The Search for the Christian Doctrine of God*, 6; Davis, *The First Seven Ecumenical Councils*, 51–53.

59. Erhman, *Christianity in Late Antiquity*, 167.

60. Lohse, *A Short History of Christian Doctrine*, 49; Fairbairn, *Life in the Trinity*, 45.

61. Lohse, *A Short History of Christian Doctrine*, 48.

May to July A.D. 325, was attended by approximately 300 bishops, called together by Emperor Constantine. No official description of the proceedings exists. In addition to the christological issue, the Council addressed numerous jurisdictional matters and other directives to the churches, and, thus, we can only reconstruct from fragmentary accounts the content of the course of the theological debate. But the outcome is clear. It boiled down to which choice of terms was more appropriate to describe the relationship of the Son to the Father: the terms *homoiousios* (of "like" or "similar" substance, preferred by the Arians), and *homoousios* (of the same substance, as advocated by Athanasius and his supporters). It was the latter term that was incorporated into the Nicene Creed: "We believe in one Lord, Jesus Christ, the only Son of God, eternally begotten of the Father, God from God, Light from Light, True God from True God, begotten, not made, of one being [*homoousios*] with the Father." The creed formulated at Nicaea was not the final formulation, but rather a first ecumenical effort in combating Arianism. The creed itself underwent a number of revisions in order to counter the ever-changing forms of Arianism. It was amplified and found its final form at the Council of Constantinople in A.D. 381. Paradoxically, immediately following Nicaea, Arianism, supposedly the loser at the Council, received a surge of support that lingered for a few centuries.[62]

The fact that Arianism continued to spread after Nicaea has several probable causes: For one, the heat of the dispute having cooled off, the amount of thought given to the issue decreased dramatically, and so many Christians just passively accepted the Arian heresy. Furthermore, since Nicaea made some unpopular rulings concerning other matters, there was a general anti-Nicene attitude, which included defying its theological decree.[63] Nevertheless, the struggle for theological clarity borne in the fourth century was not a result of widespread doctrinal confusion, per se. It was a struggle principally centered on linguistic and semantic differences rather than substantively differing doctrines. Still, Arius sought to defend his understanding of orthodoxy by establishing a genuinely competing understanding of Christ as creature. Yet, by the close of the fourth century, heresy did not derail orthodoxy but instead served as the stimulus for doctrinal clarification.[64]

---

62. Chadwick, *The Early Church*, 133.

63. Ferguson, *Church History: Volume I*, 200.

64. Gonzalez, *The Story of Christianity: Volume I*, 162–167.

THE POST-NICENE FATHERS

Gregory of Nyssa

Gregory (A.D. 335–386) penned his work *On Not Three Gods* in response to the claim that Christians worshiped three gods. In the text, he confronts those failing to acknowledge a distinction between the conceptual persons of the Trinity and the linguistic descriptions of those persons.[65] In effect, he accomplishes what Tertullian could not. As Lewis Ayers has demonstrated, for Gregory, the seemingly three separate works of the Godhead only appear as such; they are actually a single work flowing from a single essence.[66] Gregory summarizes this position by describing the power and activities of God coming from the Father as water comes from a spring. Even so, it is the Son who brings what is seen into operation and it is the power of the Spirit who acts in perfecting grace (Tres dii, 334).

Interestingly enough, it is argued that Gregory of Nyssa differs from other church fathers who see the unity of the Godhead being grounded in the Father. Rather, Gregory sees unity being based in the Father but completed or upheld in the Spirit.[67] Although Gregory does employ a variety of analogical and descriptive terminologies in assessing the power and action of the Godhead, in no way does he conceive a division in their essence. For him, the Godhead is not a partnership, but an absolute unity.[68] In the final estimation, it would seem that Gregory's argument is that while the actions of the Godhead could appear to demonstrate three gods, this assumption comes from a misunderstanding of the triune nature. Rather than defining themselves individually as do human persons, the persons of the Trinity are distinguished by different roles, yet their actions are wholly indivisible. In short, although distinctions exist among the persons, the persons are not separate individuals acting as one. They are, in actuality, one being.

Augustine

In Western Christianity (i.e. as opposed to Eastern Orthodoxy), the Trinity is definitively expressed in the works of Augustine of Hippo (A.D. 354–430);

65. Ayers, *Nicaea and its Legacy*, 347.

66. Ibid, 348.

67. Maspero, *Trinity and Man*, 179–180.

68. Ayers, *Nicaea and its Legacy*, 360.

some people would say more so than by any other author. Augustine describes the Father and the Son as distinct from one another, yet entirely unified when he writes of the Father and Son being not just one in but actually being one greatness, truth, and wisdom. Moreover, Augustine goes on to clarify that the Father and Son are distinct. They are not both the Word or the Son but remain distinct in the midst of unity (Trin., 7:1.3). Continuing this pattern of thought, Augustine writes that the Son is distinct from the Father in person but is in all things like the Father and equal to the Father. Augustine conveys this equality in deity by stating that if the Father is God then the Son is God. If the Father is Light then the Son is Light. If the Father is Wisdom then the Son is Wisdom. This unity of qualitative descriptions is true because the Father and Son are of one essence or substance. That is to say that everything the Father is as deity the Son is also. Still, the Son is not the Father and the Father is not the Son. In Augustine's theology, they are wholly distinct but entirely one (Trin., 15:14.23). This oneness and distinction is tied in large part to Augustine's theology of the Spirit. As J.N.D. Kelly has described, despite being mystified regarding the procession of the Holy Spirit, Augustine is certain that the person of the Spirit acts as the bond of love or communion between the Father and the Son (Trin., 5.12; 5.15–17), and that he proceeds from both of them.[69]

For Augustine, deity is not attributed to any one person of the Trinity. Rather, in so far as each person is a person, as the Trinity they are deity.[70] This is due to their co-equal sharing of divine attributes (Trin., 5.9). So, deity for Augustine is inextricably tied to a single, shared, divine triune nature rather than a mere combination of divine individuals.[71] This emphasis serves to maintain clarity regarding the unity of persons, rather than elevating the distinctions between the persons beyond that with which would accord with monotheism.[72]

In his book of Confessions, Augustine presents a case for God's simplicity and immutability (Conf., 4.16.28). In another work, he states that God is three persons, yet a single essence; therefore, one should not think of three gods, but a triunity (Fid.et Symb., 9). Lewis Ayers has noted that Augustine cannot envision anything but three co-eternal and co-substantial persons. That is to say, in no way does Augustine believe that the divine

---

69. Kelly, *Early Christian Doctrines*, 275; Augustine, *On the Holy Trinity*, 5.12–17.
70. Hill, *The History of Christian Thought*, 87.
71. Hill, *The History of Christian Thought*, 87.
72. Ibid, 88.

essence or being gives rise to the persons, but that the plurality of persons are intrinsic to the divine being.[73]

While Augustine's assertions are certainly true and aid in clarifying the orthodox position, his greatest contribution to Trinitarian discourse is his use of analogy. Of all his analogies, the most valuable is his picture of love. Motivated by a question about the Trinity posed by one of his students,[74] the latter Augustine begins to see the Trinity as the model for all relationships and specifically, love.[75] Augustine demonstrates that love requires no less than three aspects: "When I, who make this inquiry, love anything, there are three things concerned—myself, and that which I love, and love itself" (Trin., 9.2). The Father, Son, and Holy Spirit are analogous to one who loves, the one being loved, and the power of love.[76] This analogy is useful as there is one substance, love, but three distinct aspects of that love, all of which are necessary for love to exist. A further analogy utilized by Augustine is that of the mind. In Augustine's estimation, the Trinity could be likened to the workings of a mind. In brief, the inner workings of the Triune God are analogous to *memoria, intellegentia,* and *voluntas.*[77] The Father, Son, and Spirit interact in a manner likened to memories, wisdom, and exertion of the will. For Augustine, both the unity of the persons and their distinctions are demonstrated by the analogy of the mind. In the mind there are specific operations or processes that occur, which are distinct from another; however, not one of these processes could occur apart from the mind. Thus, with the mind there is memory, wisdom, or will. Yet, memory itself is not mind, nor is wisdom or will. Therefore, the unity of the mind with its distinct operations is, for Augustine, analogous to the nature of the Trinity.[78]

SUMMARY OF EARLY TRINITARIAN THOUGHT

The purpose of this exploration in early Trinitarian thought is to establish how early in the history of the church, nascent or proto-Nicene orthodoxy developed. It has been demonstrated that the doctrine of the Trinity in its

73. Ayers, *Nicaea and its Legacy,* 381.

74. Stump and Kretzmann, *The Cambridge Companion to Augustine,* 92.

75. Smither, *Augustine as Mentor,* 219–220.

76. Rusch, *The Trinitarian Controversy,* 26; Ayers, *Nicaea and its Legacy,* 283–284.

77. Morgan, *The Incarnation of the Word,* 30.

78. Ibid; Ayers, *Nicaea and its Legacy,* 275–296.

creedal form evolved slowly and gained clarity as time progressed. During the apostolic period, Clement and Ignatius penned letters to remedy issues within the church. Despite the fact that each stresses the unity and deity of the individual members of the divine triad, their views are still primitive and lack a conceptual explanation of God's triunity. With the advent of the Apologists, greater attention is given to the nature of the triune Godhead. Defending the deity of Christ in the face of Greek philosophy and heretical movements, Justin Martyr and Irenaeus utilize the *logos* concept. While the *logos* was beneficial in explaining the eternal nature of Christ and his procession from the Father, it does not provide the detail needed to explicate the economic nature of the triune God. It was at this juncture that Tertullian introduces terminology describing the economy of the Trinity.

Tertullian's teaching lays the groundwork for the language used within the Nicene Creed. This language proved advantageous in combating the heretical doctrines of the presbyter Arius. Much of what the council concluded to constitute orthodoxy comes as a product of the previous century's struggle with clarifying the nature of the triune God. Even though Nicaea is significant in thwarting the heresy of Arius, it serves mostly to solidify the lines of theological divide.[79] The greatest expression of Trinitarian theology was still to come in the works of Augustine. For the first time, a theologian would paint an unambiguous word picture of God's triunity. Employing a vast array of analogies, Augustine succeeds where others fall short, describing the necessity of God's triune nature.

Summarizing much of the balancing act that took place in Trinitarian development during the early church (and throughout the rest of church history), Allan Coppedge notes that early Trinitarians travelled a narrow theological course between two pitfalls.[80] First, there was a potential over-emphasis upon the distinction in persons within the Godhead that could lead to tritheism. This theological danger was very real and ever-present in the early church due to the pagan context in which Christian theology was being explained and espoused. The guardrail for the early church (and modern Nicene Christians) in preventing tritheism was the monotheism of the Old Testament. Yet, this adherence to monotheism also provided an avenue for error. In an attempt to prevent a lapse into tritheism, there was a tendency toward modalism. So, throughout the writings of the early church

---

79. Erhman, *Christianity in Late Antiquity*, 157.
80. Coppedge, *The God Who is Triune*, 82.

fathers, there is an evident attempt to find a biblical balance between the oneness of God and the plurality of person.

In conclusion, in order to fully appreciate historic, orthodox Christianity one must examine the historical development of its doctrine of God. Such an investigation should focus upon the patristic struggle to formulate an orthodox creed that expresses the triunity of God without violating Christianity's commitment to monotheism.[81] The early church did not engage in speculative theology in order to develop Trinitarian convictions; rather, they simply developed an understanding of God that was faithful to the Scriptures' teaching that there is but one God and He is three persons. In short, the data engaged in this chapter thus far answer the first of two research questions that necessitate the writing of this chapter as whole: What is the historical, orthodox position on the Trinity and how early was it established? What has been demonstrated is that proto-Nicene orthodoxy becomes evident in the writings of the church fathers by the late first or early second centuries.

CONCLUSION

The aim of this chapter has been to answer the following research questions: What is the historical, orthodox position on the Trinity, and how early was it established? Only by engaging with primary sources from the early church fathers can the first question be adequately addressed. A synopsis of the detailed interaction with the early church, supplied throughout this chapter, will be provided below. This information is necessary for understanding Nicene orthodoxy in the history of the church and especially among contemporary theologians. It is only by understanding orthodoxy prior to Joseph Smith that his theology can be assessed from a historical perspective. Thus, the data contained in this chapter demonstrate the historical basis upon which to engage Smith's tritheism.

To reiterate the content of this chapter, for Nicene Christians, the doctrine of the Trinity is clearly taught within Scripture. The ensuing Trinitarian creedal formulations resulted from historical meditation upon the Scriptures. When the church was born, she eagerly awaited the return of Jesus Christ. The expectation of the early church was that Christ would return within the lifetime of those who had seen Him ministering on earth. This conviction precluded any significant theological exploration. However,

81. Ibid, 27.

the rise of various heretical groups pushed forward the development of standards for orthodoxy. Out of this theological progression came descriptions and defenses that demonstrated the coherence of a triune God. These data have served to answer one of the primary research questions of this project: What is the historical, orthodox position on the Trinity and how early was it established? The information provided in this chapter revealed that although creedal Trinitarianism developed steadily from the second to fourth centuries, nascent Trinitarianism was present in the writings of Christian thinkers immediately following the close of the New Testament era.

While the information presented in this chapter goes further in answering the research questions motivating this project, there are still more questions to be explored. Many of the remaining questions focus upon Joseph Smith, his context, theology, and the results of his theology. The next chapter will begin (in light of the data presented in the present chapter) to examine the theological context in which Joseph Smith broke from Nicene orthodoxy and developed his own brand of tritheism.

Chapter 4

Joseph Smith's Historical Context

INTRODUCTION

The previous chapter traces the development of Nicene orthodoxy leading up to the time of Augustine of Hippo. The purpose of the present chapter is to answer the following two research questions: First, what was the historical context in which Joseph Smith formulated his tritheism? Second, in what manner did Joseph Smith's theological environment encourage theological innovation? In order to address these questions properly, orthodoxy in the eighteenth-century North American context has to be engaged. These data will establish that the rise of revolutionary ideals among the colonies coincided with a growing sense of theological freedom apart from historic, Nicene orthodoxy. This process sets the stage for the varying influences upon Joseph Smith's life and theological development. The potential and even probable influences upon Joseph Smith's theology and self-designation as a prophet will be demonstrated to be quite numerous.

THE OVERALL RELIGIOUS ENVIRONMENT

The Eighteenth Century Setting

It must be stated from the outset that at numerous times throughout history, those seeking freedom have often been associated with theology that at least appeared to be unorthodox. Prior to the establishment of the colonies in the New World, religious oppression at the hands of the state was a common occurrence in Europe. Furthermore, quite often, those groups most devout in espousing the virtue of liberty were outside of the mainstream of Nicene Christianity. For instance, the Quakers of Germany held to a belief in continuing revelation, and as result found themselves under pressure from Lutheran churches in the region.[1] Because of this persecution from churches sanctioned by the state (in Germany and elsewhere), William Penn wrote an essay on religious liberty, proposing the need for separation between governmental and ecclesiastical authority.[2] Eventually, the Quakers began immigrating en masse to colonize Pennsylvania, in the hope of finding religious freedom.

Throughout the Old World, religious persecution against Protestant groups abounded. Roman Catholicism sought to squelch the spread of the Reformation through governmental processes.[3] Interestingly, those same Protestants who sought freedom from the oppression of Roman Catholicism and the Church of England, after rising to dominance in a region, often established equally oppressive regimes.[4] Moreover, upon reaching the New World for the purpose of freely expressing their religion apart from the regulation of Old World authorities, many groups (including the Puritans) established their own blending of ecclesiastical and governmental powers.[5] These authorities, although generally localized, were rather hostile to belief systems outside of their understanding of Nicene Christianity.[6] Further complicating the matter was the perceived excesses in religion that occurred in colonies holding to absolute religious liberty, such as Rhode

---

1. Sweet, *The Story of Religion in America*, 23.

2. Cairns, *Christianity Through the Centuries*, 363; Noll, *A History of Christianity in the United States and Canada*, 65; Sweet, *The Story of Religion in America*, 23.

3. Cairns, *Christianity Through the Centuries*, 343–346.

4. Ibid, 347.

5. Ibid, 358–361; Noll, *A History of Christianity in the United States and Canada*, 41–53; Sweet, *The Story of Religion in America*, 50–51.

6. Noll, *A History of Christianity in the United States and Canada*, 65.

Island.[7] Thus, while many came to the New World in search of religious freedom, the colonies were still permeated with a blend of religious and governmental authority meant to uphold historic, Nicene orthodoxy.[8] The general perception among those endorsing a restrained form of religious freedom was that those who allowed any and all religious expression gave occasion to unorthodox expressions of Christianity.[9]

During the middle of the seventeenth century, Old World institutions holding to Nicene orthodoxy flourished in the colonies, especially Virginia.[10] In fact, at the middle of the eighteenth century, Virginia alone had thirty Anglican churches.[11] By the close of the century, that number would rise to over sixty.[12] Still, Anglicanism did not hold absolute theological sway over the colonies. As the eighteenth century began to take shape, an influx of Baptists, Methodists, and Presbyterians began to spread throughout the colonies.[13]

The growth of these Protestant groups was due in large part to the Declaration of Religious Toleration issued by William and Mary in 1689.[14] This declaration ensured the general right of individuals to worship as they see fit. Differing from Anglicanism on a number of points (i.e. state-sanctioned religion), these Protestant groups remained solidly committed to historic orthodoxy.[15] However, it should be noted that the assertion that the colonies represented a "Christian America" is patently false. In fact, prior to the Great Awakening, the number of colonial citizens who were members of local churches hovered around no more than twenty percent of the population.[16] In spite of the rather low percentage of citizens faithfully attending church, the Protestant movement that exerted the greatest level of theological influence over the colonies was that of Puritanism.[17]

---

7. Gaustad, *A Religious History of America*, 71.

8. See Cornett, *Christian America?*, 2011.

9. Gaustad, *A Religious History of America*, 71.

10. Ibid, 45; Noll, *America's God*, 20.

11. Gaustad, *A Religious History of America*, 45.

12. Ibid.

13. Ibid, 46.

14. Ibid; Beneke, *Beyond Toleration*, 33–34.

15. Noll, *America's God*, 19–30.

16. Sweet, *The Story of Religion in America*, 5.

17. Noll, *America's God*, 19.

Puritanism

Perhaps the primary reason for the influence of the Puritans over the colonies at-large has to do with the sheer number of their published works. More than any other North American group at the time, the Puritan thinkers throughout New England wrote and published books and pamphlets that espoused a staunchly orthodox, Calvinist theology.[18] While some theological particulars differed from one Puritan theologian to another, Calvinistic theology, rooted in Augustinian thought, remained the anchor of all Puritan theology.[19]

Not all Puritans were academics, but the most influential and outspoken Puritans were generally well educated.[20] This emphasis upon the role of the mind in a Christian society led the Puritans to develop highly detailed doctrinal treatises, along with rigorous catechetical procedures.[21] The influence of Puritan theology and lifestyle practices cannot be overstated. By the time of the American Revolution, Sydney Ahlstrom argues that close to three-fourths of the colonial population had been influenced in some manner by Puritanism.[22] Therefore, the theological landscape of this period was largely dominated by Nicene orthodoxy.

The Great Awakening

Interestingly enough, the period that marked the collapse of Puritan influence and theological sway was a time of revival centered upon the very doctrines espoused by the Puritans. This time of revival, called the "Great Awakening," began to take shape late in the winter of 1734. Under the preaching of Jonathan Edwards (1703–1758), a devout Trinitarian,[23] the church in Northampton, Massachusetts experienced a renewed response to the gospel message.[24] By early 1735, the enthusiasm experienced in Northampton for the gospel had spread to surrounding towns and

18. Ibid, 21.

19. Ibid.

20. Ahlstrom, *A Religious History of the American People*, 130.

21. Ibid.

22. Ibid, 124.

23. Edwards, *The Works of Jonathan Edwards: Volume 2*, 109–148.

24. Gonzalez, *The Story of Christianity: Volume II*, 228.

counties.[25] Declining sharply after its peak in the spring of 1735, the revival (witnessed and perhaps instigated by Jonathan Edwards) spread across twenty-five communities in Massachusetts and Connecticut.[26] By 1737, the frontier revival, as Edwards called it, had waned significantly.[27] It was at this time that Edwards penned an account of the revival entitled A *Faithful Narrative of the Surprising Work of God*.[28]

Following the publications of Edwards' account of the revival, George Whitefield (1715–1770) returned to the colonies from England. Sharing Edwards' commitment to historic orthodoxy, and specifically Reformed theology,[29] Whitefield commenced a preaching tour that would take him from New York to Georgia.[30] Whitefield's energetic preaching, coupled with the expectations that flowed from the publication of Edwards' narrative, led to anticipation for revival among many colonists, especially New Englanders.[31] Whitefield's preaching tour through the New England colonies and the South, and the resultant revivals, led to a growing sense of commonality among the colonies, as well as deep interest in spiritual matters.[32]

The results of both Edwards' and Whitefield's revivals were transformative for the colonies for a number of reasons. First, there was a development of an attitude of disregard for established church traditions.[33] More than Edwards, Whitefield typified this attitude in both his preaching style and his evangelistic methodology.[34] Even though Edwards marked a break from some of the traditions of the Puritanical past in New England, it was largely Whitefield who brought a radically new approach to both preaching and church life to the forefront.[35]

---

25. Noll, *The Rise of Evangelicalism*, 77–78; Latourette, *A History of Christianity: Volume II*, 959.

26. Kidd, *The Great Awakening*, 21; Ahlstrom, *A Religious History of the American People*, 282–283.

27. Ibid; Hill, *Zondervan Handbook to the History of Christianity*, 332.

28. Kidd, *The Great Awakening*, 13–21.

29. Gonzalez, *The Story of Christianity: Volume II*, 228–229.

30. Ahlstrom, *A Religious History of the American People*, 283; Latourette, *A History of Christianity: Volume II*, 959.

31. Kidd, *The Great Awakening*, 22; Ahlstrom, *A Religious History of the American People*, 287.

32. Gonzalez, *The Story of Christianity: Volume II*, 229–230.

33. Noll, *The Rise of Evangelicalism*, 107.

34. Ibid.

35. Ahlstrom, *A Religious History of the American People*, 286–287.

The second notable outcome of the Great Awakening, as led by Edwards and Whitefield, was a splintering of ecclesiastical structuring.[36] Given the themes of revival preaching, especially in the case of Edwards, there arose a variety of approaches in how to understand "church." For some, a separatist path seemed necessary, while for others a more social approach to understanding the covenant that defines a church body was a more suitable course. In short, in the wake of Edwards' and Whitefield's preaching, the traditional church structure ceased to dominate the New England landscape.[37]

The third most pertinent effect of the Great Awakening, for the purpose of this research, was a new American religious ideal. While the Puritans of the past sought to establish a deep, rigid theology founded upon the content of Nicene orthodoxy, many coming out of the Great Awakening were drawn to what could be called a "Christian Republicanism."[38] As will be explored, the blending of republicanism and theology gave rise to a volatile mix of political, social, and religious thought that contributed to both the American Revolution and theological innovation.[39]

"Christian Republicanism"

In the decades leading up to the Great Awakening, there were clear and significant divides among churches and denominations.[40] Essentially, prior to the efforts of Edwards and Whitefield to establish the gospel message as the dividing line among churches, there was a considerable disconnect even among Protestants. Following the Great Awakening, a new level of cooperation began to develop among many, but not all, Protestants.[41]

This new cooperation paralleled the political sentiments among many colonists. If republicanism represented a united, political resistance to British tyranny, Christian Republicanism represented both a sanctified form of political resistance, as well as an aversion to the perceived tyranny of

36. Noll, *America's God*, 48–49; Sweet, *The Story of Religion in America*, 134.

37. Noll, *America's God*, 48–49.

38. Sandoz, *Republicanism, Religion, and the Soul of America*, 6; Noll, *America's God*, 49.

39. Noll, *A History of Christianity in the United States and Canada*, 116.

40. Sweet, *The Story of Religion in America*, 172.

41. Sandoz, *Republicanism, Religion, and the Soul of America*, 57; Sweet, *The Story of Religion in America*, 172.

traditional religious institutions.[42] In essence, the Great Awakening ushered the colonies, especially in the Northeast, away from traditional religion grounded in institutions. In place of institutional religion, there arose individual expressions of religiosity, embracing emerging modernist thought. Such a transition had far-reaching effects.[43]

First, religion became seen as something to be driven by laity rather than clergy.[44] Second, there emerged a tendency to view piety and religiosity as of greater value than doctrinal precision or clarity.[45] The appearance of a religious environment in opposition to established orthodoxy is not surprising, considering the fact that throughout history, religious institutions in subordination to the state have tended to blend into tyrannical systems.[46] In the context of Old World religion, governmental powers aligned themselves with either the Church of England, the Lutheran synods, Reformed authorities, or Roman Catholicism. Essentially, if one were to express religious beliefs outside those sanctioned by these institutions, governmental as well as ecclesiastical retribution, would likely occur.[47] Thus, the doctrinal emphasis of powerful, civil, religious and state religious movements became suspect in a post-Great Awakening, colonial America.[48] This scenario inspired attitudes of religious freedom from both institutional and doctrinal constraint in a similar fashion to the freedom from political oppression that the colonists pursued.[49] While only in limited form, during this period in colonial America there were some state-sanctioned religious entities. However, with the rise of republicanism and in light of what occurred in the Great Awakening, there arose an organized body of religious dissenters who desired to see the colonies institute laws guaranteeing the individual freedom of citizens to choose their own religion.[50]

---

42. Noll, *America's God,* 55; Sweet, *The Story of Religion in America,* 172; Latourette, *A History of Christianity: Volume II,* 961–963.

43. Kidd, *God of Liberty,* 21; Noll, *America's God,* 4.

44. McLoughlin, "The Role of Religion in the Revolution," 150; Noll, *America's God,* 44; Beneke, *Beyond Toleration,* 53–56.

45. Noll, *America's God,* 44.

46. Gaustad, *Faiths of our Fathers,* 6.

47. Kidd, *God of Liberty,* 20.

48. Gaustad, *Faiths of our Fathers,* 6.

49. Ibid; McLoughlin, "The Role of Religion in the Revolution," 149.

50. Lambert, *Founding Fathers and the Place of Religion in America,* 208.

What was once a political desire for liberty took on a religious exuberance. This attitude made the cause of freedom from governmental oppression also a movement bent on dismantling ecclesiastical institutions deemed oppressive in some form or another.[51] Nathan O. Hatch described this sentiment as "Civil Millennialism," meaning that American freedom was seen as on a par with the commencement of the millennial reign of Christ.[52] What typified the Civil Millennialist ideology was a move away from seeing the evangelization of the world as the chief goal of the Christian religion, and in its place the dismantling of tyrannical powers, be they governmental or religious.[53]

Those who opposed the assimilation of religion into republicanism as a political theory did so because they believed that this approach to society and religion would undermine historic, orthodox Christian doctrine.[54] These concerns seemed justified when orthodox Christians, who became ardent supporters of republicanism, began to disavow historic orthodox doctrines such as the Trinity. Moreover, popular publications, stressing the virtue of republicanism, advocated abandoning religious dogma in favor of autonomous human reason.[55]

J.C.D. Clark has documented the connection between republicanism and anti-orthodox religious movements at length. As he observed, there is an undeniable link between unorthodox, anti-orthodox, and heterodox religious movements and republicanism.[56] Given the subject of the present research, Joseph Smith's tritheism, it is significant that there is a historical connection to the rise of republicanism in colonial America with Arianism, Socinianism, and Deism.[57] All of these systems are vehemently opposed to historic Nicene orthodoxy on the deity of Christ and the doctrine of the Trinity.

As stated in the previous chapter, Arianism proposed that God the Son is not eternal; rather, He is the first created being.[58] Taking for granted

51. Hatch, "The Origins of Civil Millennialism in America," 87.

52. Ibid, 86.

53. Ibid, 87; Hatch, "Visions of a Republican Millennium," 162; Kidd, *God of Liberty*, 16; Sandoz, *Republicanism, Religion, and the Soul of America*, 17–18.

54. Noll, *America's God*, 56–58.

55. Ibid, 59–61.

56. Clark, *The Language of Liberty 1660–1832*, 38–39.

57. Ibid.

58. Hanson, *The Search for the Christian Doctrine of God*, 6; Davis, *The First Seven*

that the previous chapter engaged with Arianism and its founder, Arius, it would be prudent to briefly explore what is meant by Socinianism and Deism. Both of these systems assume Unitarianism, which is the belief that God is not just one being but also one person.[59] Socinianism began as a reaction to the Protestant Reformation. Its founder, Faustus Socinus (1539-1604), was firmly committed to traditional orthodox beliefs such as the virgin birth of Jesus and the reliability of Scripture. However, he ardently opposed the historic, Nicene position on the doctrine of the Trinity.[60] Instead, Socinus believed in a fallible, monadic God who lacked foreknowledge and the ability to create ex nihilo.[61]

Similar to Socinianism in its denial of the Trinity, Deism is a little more difficult to define. As a system, Deism does not appear consistently throughout history. The Deism referenced in this research is a specific form that gained popularity in the seventeenth and eighteenth centuries.[62] Among many of the leading thinkers behind republicanism and the ideas of liberty that undergirded the American Revolution, there was a belief in a sort of divine "watchmaker" (i.e. intelligent creator), who is a solitary person, not directly connected to the world.[63]

Among the Founding Fathers there were a variety of approaches to Deism. For John Locke (not a founding father himself, but a philosopher who had great influence on them), the solitary divine person could reveal Himself via special revelation but remained distant from the created world.[64] Benjamin Franklin went beyond Locke in ascribing a level of knowability to the divine person in such a manner that he should be worshiped in some fashion or form.[65] Certainly more could be said about both Deism and Socinianism, but the core content of their systems is what must be emphasized: both of them (along with Arianism) denied Nicene orthodoxy as it related to the doctrine of the Trinity. Given the penchant appeal of republicanism to those who advocated unorthodox and heretical positions

---

Ecumenical Councils, 51–53.

59. Gomes, *Unitarian Universalism*, 9.

60. Ibid, 42–53.

61. Ibid, 40.

62. Cairns, *Christianity Through the Centuries*, 379–380; Sire, *The Universe Next Door*, 50.

63. Latourette, *A History of Christianity: Volume II*, 1006–1007.

64. Sire, *The Universe Next Door*, 49–50.

65. Holmes, *The Faiths of the Founding Fathers*, 55.

on the nature of God, the concern of orthodox religious institutions regarding the pervasiveness of republicanism becomes quite understandable.[66]

Going further, the development of republicanism and its mingling with religion, led directly to an anticlerical attitude among the leadership of those dissenting from England.[67] There was a general suspicion of those representing established, orthodox religion because of historical connections between Nicene Christianity and those leading tyrannical regimes.[68] Thus, organized religion with its emphasis upon established dogma became somewhat of a specter of tyranny in the minds of many colonists.

It would seem that what contributed to this suspicion was the blending of multiple ideologies into an American, republican movement. Leading up to the American Revolution, the idea of religious tolerance shifted from mere tolerance to absolute freedom and individual autonomy. This notion became blended with the ideal of individual liberty as it related to established, governmental influence. So, what were at one point parallel ideas of freedom became blended into a new American virtue that espoused contempt for beliefs or lifestyles imposed by outside forces.[69]

American Religion and the Revolution

As indicated by the background information previously assessed, the intellectual and theological currents giving occasion to the American Revolution were turning into a religiously unstable mix. So, what exactly did Christianity look like in a theological sense at the time of the American Revolution? What trends had emerged?

Even though many churches and denominations continued to maintain the key elements of Nicene orthodoxy, a great deal of theological innovation began to take shape in the decades surrounding the American Revolution.[70] Among the Congregationalists arose a faction intent on breaking from Reformed theology and moving toward a more liberal

---

66. Noll, *America's God*, 63.

67. Robbins, *The Eighteenth Century Commonwealthman*, 116.

68. Ibid, 124; Lambert, *Founding Fathers and the Place of Religion in America*, 207.

69. Hatch, *The Democratisation of American Christianity*, 6–7; Noll, *A History of Christianity in the United States and Canada*, 151–152.

70. Latourette, *A History of Christianity: Volume II*, 1007; Noll, *America's God*, 114–138.

understanding of Christian doctrine.[71] The changes that occurred were, first, a rejection of the necessity of special revelation for knowing God, found in the Christian Scripture.[72] Second, there was a renewed belief in the goodness of humanity and its ability to determine its own spiritual fate.[73] Third, the liberal Congregationalists espoused a new way of interpreting Scripture designed to free the reader from the constraints of context and historic interpretations.[74]

In broad terms, there was an increasing, populist disdain for the recitation of and adherence to "inherited creeds" of Christendom.[75] Such an attitude called traditional doctrine and orthodoxy into question in light of revolutionary ideals. Early in the present chapter, the effects of the Great Awakening were presented as contributing to some of the theological trends being discussed. The connection becomes all the more clear when it is noted that many of the unorthodox theological trends of the revolutionary period were instigated by those directly influenced by the Great Awakening. For instance, leaders within the Shakers and Universalist movements had been "converted" under the preaching of George Whitefield.[76] In evaluating the overall themes that remained constant throughout the theology of these Great Awakening converts, Mark Noll notes that one constant is a belief in the continuing occurrence of special revelation.[77] These theological innovators generally advocated a belief in special revelation occurring outside the text of traditional Scripture and being ascertained by spiritual practices, dreams, visions, and hermetic rituals.[78]

Sydney Ahlstrom has identified a number of growing theological tendencies during the revolutionary era. In his estimation, the theological innovations of the period were marked by the desire for redefinition. Ahlstrom sees the first of these reformulations coming in the form of an

71. Noll, *America's God*, 139.

72. Ibid.

73. Ibid.

74. Ibid, 140–141.

75. Ibid, 151.

76. Gutek and Gutek, *Visiting Utopian Communities*, 32–33; Foster, *Religion and Sexuality*, 270.

77. Noll, *America's God*, 154.

78. Gutek and Gutek, *Visiting Utopian Communities*, 40; Foster, *Religion and Sexuality*, 66–67; Noll, *America's God*, 154.

outright Arminian insistence upon the inherent goodness of mankind.[79] This insistence produced a theological bias in which it was assumed that the will of the individual is the defining factor for redemption. Further, a common theme in theological reformulations relied heavily upon the assumption that history, tradition, and creeds were of little value.[80] The institutions that proposed adherence to such ideas were considered suspect. Additionally, a widespread theological emphasis was a move away from understanding God as Trinity and to merely the "Deity."[81]

During the period immediately following the American Revolution, traditional religious institutions affirming Nicene orthodoxy experienced a depression of sorts.[82] The colonial interest in established religion began to wane from what Sydney Ahlstrom describes as "spiritual exhaustion."[83] So, while new religious freedom and republican ideals called into question traditional institutions of government and religion, including religious doctrine, theological innovation flourished throughout the newly formed nation.

In the decades following the American Revolution there emerged a new religious vigor among those throughout New England.[84] However, this did not translate into a new commitment to historic, Nicene Christianity. By the close of the revolutionary era, only about twenty percent of the population, across the newly formed nation, were members of churches in the Nicene tradition.[85] This was due in part to the negative sentiments that developed throughout the revolutionary period toward the idea of a single religious orthodoxy dominating a people or region.[86] In fact, the general feeling of the American public at-large was negative towards what was seen as the "heavy hand" of historic, Nicene religion.[87] The consequence of these trends in public feeling was the rise of anti-Trinitarian thought among

---

79. Ahlstrom, *A Religious History of the American People*, 356–357.

80. Ibid.

81. Ibid, 358. Cairns, *Christianity Through the Centuries*, 429.

82. Ahlstrom, *A Religious History of the American People*, 365.

83. Ibid.

84. Butler et al., *Religion in American Life*, 142; Latourette, *A History of Christianity: Volume II*, 1037.

85. Butler et al., *Religion in American Life*, 145.

86. Ibid, 158.

87. Ibid, 165; Latourette, *A History of Christianity: Volume II*, 1035.

many in academia. Moreover, it encouraged some to pursue non-tradition-al religious expressions outside of the bounds of Nicene orthodoxy.[88]

Summary

The early colonial period of American history was dominated by the theo-logical influence of the Puritans. This is not to say that every so-called Christian or church followed in the Puritan heritage of Reformed doctrine or Nicene orthodoxy; rather, the prevailing theological frame of late sev-enteenth and early eighteenth century theology was generally Nicene. The Great Awakening brought with it a resurgence of appreciation for Christian doctrine, and even historic Nicene orthodoxy. However, the Great Awaken-ing also gave rise to a new, personal way of viewing religion. This situation deadened the sense of necessary adherence to the orthodoxy that existed in communities of faith. This scenario was further complicated by the surge of republicanism. Although republicanism espoused the freedom of religion, it carried with it an incipient disdain for established, historic Christian in-stitutions and teachings. So, as the enthusiasm for political freedom reached a fever pitch, the distrust of established, Nicene orthodoxy also grew. Even-tually, for many in the general population, a skepticism developed toward all things associated with tyrannical rule, even Nicene orthodoxy as seen in the established church.

This information provides a necessary introduction to the world in which Joseph Smith would develop his theology. Further, these data answer the first research question motivating this chapter: What was the historical context in which Joseph Smith formulated his tritheism? In short, Joseph Smith was born shortly after a period of major religious upheaval that led to a growing lack of commitment to Nicene orthodoxy. Further, the new emphasis upon personal religion, anti-Trinitarian religion, and freedom to create new religious societies provided fertile ground in which to develop innovative and ultimately anti-Nicene theology.

JOSEPH SMITH'S CONTEXT AND ENVIRONMENT

The theological context in which Joseph Smith was born was undergoing drastic changes. A new emphasis upon personal religion and a move away

88. Butler et al., *Religion in American Life*, 167–168.

from institutional, Nicene orthodoxy was underway. What influence did this have upon the theological development of Joseph Smith? While there is no definitive answer to this question, probable influences can be discerned.

Joseph Smith's Family

Joseph Smith's Grandparents

Certainly, Joseph Smith's family life influenced his theological development. So, what exactly did Smith's family believe about God? Were they aligned with Nicene orthodoxy? Joseph's mother, Lucy Mack Smith (1775–1856), was born to Solomon and Lydia Mack. Lucy recounted that Solomon Mack was driven by the desire to be wealthy.[89] Spending most of Lucy's formative years away from home, Solomon bounced from one business venture to another in an attempt to obtain riches. At the age of fifty-six, Solomon returned home to his family on a permanent basis.[90] Throughout his life, Solomon was prone to experience "fits," as he ambiguously described these events, which were probably some form of seizure.[91] Despite growing up rather free of religious influences, late in his life Solomon experienced some form of religious conversion.[92] Following this conversion, Solomon looked back upon his periodic fits with a new, religious understanding.

Solomon's conversion to religion was one that Fawn Brodie typified as little more than mysticism.[93] Supposedly, Solomon Mack experienced visions of lights and heard disembodied voices.[94] Such occurrences are not necessarily outside of the Nicene tradition. However, they have not been historically associated with Nicene orthodoxy.

Joseph Smith's maternal grandmother was named Lydia Mack. Along with her son Jason, she clearly exercised a great deal of influence on Joseph's mother, Lucy. Lydia, the daughter of a deacon in a congregational church, joined a congregational church shortly after marrying Solomon.[95] It was

89. Bushman, *Joseph Smith: Rough Stone Rolling*, 30.

90. Ibid, 31.

91. Riley, *The Founder of Mormonism*, 345–346; Brodie, *No Man Knows My History*, 3–4.

92. Bushman, *Joseph Smith: Rough Stone Rolling*, 31.

93. Brodie, *No Man Knows My History*, 4.

94. Ibid; Riley, *The Founder of Mormonism*, 15–16.

95. Bushman, *Joseph Smith: Rough Stone Rolling*, 33.

under her influence that the Mack children, including Lucy and Jason, were exposed to organized religion. Lucy's brother Jason (Joseph's uncle) became a self-identified religious seeker at the age of sixteen and a lay-preacher at twenty.[96] However, Jason's pursuit of religion was far outside the bounds of Nicene orthodoxy. Jason would eventually set up a small, communistic community of approximately thirty families in New Brunswick.[97]

In modern terminology, Jason Mack's religious community could be deemed as a "cult" or its alternative designation, an "alternative religious community." For the purpose of the present research, the terms cult and cultic should be defined. The designation "cult" is meant to describe an exclusivist group that has a prophetic figure in leadership who professes special or unique knowledge beyond the Christian Scriptures. This special knowledge is meant to correct traditional Christianity.[98] Generally, the social tendencies of such a group include authoritarian control by the prophetic figure, prescribed lifestyle practices, and a consistent aversion to historic, Nicene orthodoxy.[99] Groups for whom these social tendencies appear to be true, but who lack a clearly defined prophetic leader would fall under the general designation of "cultic" rather than "cult."

The reasons for categorizing Jason Mack's community in this fashion center around three facts. First, Jason Mack's followers trusted him alone as their religious authority.[100] This in itself does not mean his community was cultic. However, when coupled with the other two facts it becomes quite evident that this group could at least be described as cultic. The second reason for identifying the New Brunswick community as a cultic sect is fact that Jason Mack was given charge of the community's economic well-being.[101] That is to say that Jason Mack directed the finances of the roughly thirty families in his religious movement. Third, Jason Mack emphasized faith healing, ecstasy and spiritual gifts.[102] Beyond the data provided, not much is known of Jason Mack's religious community. However, the infor-

96. Ibid; Remini, *Joseph Smith*, 11–12; Smith, *Biographical Sketches of Joseph Smith, the Prophet*, 21–22.

97. Gibbs, *Lights and Shadows of Mormonism*, 34; Brodie, *No Man Knows My History*, 4.

98. Tucker, Another Gospel, 16.

99. Ibid.

100. Brodie, *No Man Knows My History*, 4.

101. Ibid.

102. Kauffman and Kauffman, *The Latter Day Saints*, 19–20; Bushman, *Joseph Smith: Rough Stone Rolling*, 33; Smith, *Biographical Sketches of Joseph Smith, the Prophet*, 21–22.

mation examined demonstrates that Jason Mack's efforts for establishing a new religious sect were outside of the mainstream of Nicene orthodoxy.

On his father's side, Joseph Smith's grandparents may have also had direct influence upon his eventual theological shape.[103] Joseph's grandfather Asael and his grandmother Mary were wed in 1767.[104] Asael was an American patriot, having served in the American Revolution.[105] While identifying himself as a Christian, Asael was admittedly rather irreligious.[106] Shortly after the American Revolution ended, Asael drifted away from his basically Nicene affiliation with the Topsfield Congregational Church. As Richard Bushman has noted (himself a member of the LDS church), Asael Smith moved from Nicene orthodoxy because of his affinity with the Universalist teaching of John Murray.[107] Asael became convinced that Christ died for every sinner and thereby secured their salvation, regardless of their beliefs.[108] In 1785, Murray's followers would coalesce into a movement called the Universalist Society.[109] The moderator for this new society was Asael Smith. Bushman himself has stated that Asael's family slowly moved from Universalism back to Nicene Christianity before eventually converting to Mormonism.[110] However, throughout the religious development of Asael's family, Universalism flavored all of the Smith family's religion.[111]

Joseph Smith's Parents

Provided that both of Joseph Smith's grandfathers were engaged in or interested in religious factions either outside of or opposed to Nicene orthodoxy, what effect did they have on Smith's parents? What exactly were the religious leanings of Joseph Smith Sr. (1771–1840) and Lucy Mack Smith? Was their theological affiliation different from their own parents or were they, also, outside of Nicene orthodoxy?

103. Marsh, *The Eyewitness History of the Church*, 53.

104. Bushman, *Joseph Smith: Rough Stone Rolling*, 34.

105. Ibid.

106. Brodie, *No Man Knows My History*, 2.

107. Bushman, *Joseph Smith: Rough Stone Rolling*, 36–37.

108. Ibid.

109. Ibid, 37.

110. Ibid; Cf. Remini, *Joseph Smith*, 13.

111. Kauffman and Kauffman, *The Latter Day Saints*, 18.

In her own history of her son, Lucy Mack Smith attested that even as a young woman she believed that all of the churches of her time were in error.[112] It was her conviction that all of the denominations of the day were very much unlike the early church in doctrine or practice.[113] Such was her attitude toward established Nicene Christianity prior to her marriage to Joseph Smith Sr.

Much of what is known of the elder Joseph Smith's theological ideas comes from after his marriage to Lucy Mack. As previously mentioned, Lucy was convinced that all Protestant denominations were in error of some kind. This is a sentiment generally accepted by Joseph Smith Sr.[114] He was rather indifferent to religion as an institution except for his early, albeit brief, foray into Universalism. This assessment of organized Nicene religion was exemplified in his feelings towards Lucy's involvement in the Second Great Awakening. He witnessed Lucy's engagement with the revival, but for him it demonstrated only that those immersed in organized religion knew less about the things of God than those of the "world."[115]

After a bout with illness in 1803, Lucy became preoccupied with the subject of religion.[116] She eventually found her way to a Presbyterian church, only to be dismayed that, in her opinion, the minister knew nothing of the Word of Life.[117] In time, Lucy desired to be baptized, but only did so after finding a minister willing to baptize her without the promise that she intended to align herself with a particular theology or denomination.[118] As Richard L. Bushman describes her, Lucy became a seeker after the pattern of her older brother Jason.[119]

Sometime thereafter, Lucy became interested in the revival growing among the Methodist churches.[120] Despite his aversion to religion, Joseph Smith Sr. agreed to attend a few Methodist meetings with Lucy. However,

---

112. Smith, *Biographical Sketches of Joseph Smith, the Prophet*, 36–37.

113. Ibid.

114. Kauffman and Kauffman, *The Latter Day Saints*, 17–18; Brodie, *No Man Knows My History*, 5.

115. Persuitte, *Joseph Smith and the Origins of the Book of Mormon*, 25; Bushman, *Joseph Smith: Rough Stone Rolling*, 44; Kauffman and Kauffman, *The Latter Day Saints*, 18–20; Brodie, *No Man Knows My History*, 5.

116. Remini, *Joseph Smith*, 13; Bushman, *Joseph Smith: Rough Stone Rolling*, 45.

117. Smith, *Biographical Sketches of Joseph Smith, the Prophet*, 48.

118. Ibid; Kauffman and Kauffman, *The Latter Day Saints*, 19.

119. Bushman, *Joseph Smith: Rough Stone Rolling*, 45.

120. Ibid; Brodie, *No Man Knows My History*, 5; Remini, *Joseph Smith*, 15.

Joseph Sr.'s interaction with the Methodists was brief. Shortly after hearing of his son's loose association with Methodism, Asael Smith rather angrily demanded that Joseph Sr. read Thomas Paine's Age of Reason. Asael, still associated with Universalism, believed it to be utterly unfathomable that his son could give consideration to evangelical or Nicene orthodoxy.[121]

As Joseph Sr. attended the Methodist meetings of 1810 with Lucy, he became marginally interested in religion, just not organized religion.[122] Instead, as Lucy recounts, Joseph Sr. had a series of dreams in which he believed he was given insight to understand that the religion of the day, in established (Nicene) churches, was no religion at all.[123] This attitude toward established churches would suit Lucy quite well because of her belief in a personalized religion free from the constraints of institutional dogma.[124] It was during this period of religious upheaval in the Smith home that Joseph Smith Jr. was born (December 23, 1805).

Joseph Smith's Life

His Early Years

During Joseph Smith's (1805–1844) early life, the Smith family moved often. They eventually traversed Vermont, New Hampshire, and parts of New York before finally settling near Palmyra, New York in 1816.[125] It was during these travels that his father, Joseph Smith Sr., had many of his dreams and visions that supposedly revealed the errors that the religions of the day perpetuated.[126] In fact, as Lucy Smith recounts, it was during their time in New Hampshire that Joseph Sr. had a vision in which his children participated in the downfall of spiritual Babylon (established religion).[127]

Acknowledging the Smith family's diverse and rather unorthodox theological heritage, Richard L. Bushman notes that during the Smiths' migration across Vermont, New Hampshire, and New York, Joseph Sr. began

---

121. Bushman, *Joseph Smith: Rough Stone Rolling*, 45.

122. Smith, *Biographical Sketches of Joseph Smith, the Prophet*, 55.

123. Ibid, 55–56.

124. Brodie, *No Man Knows My History*, 5.

125. Abanes, *One Nation Under Gods*, 8.

126. Remini, *Joseph Smith*, 20.

127. Smith, *Biographical Sketches of Joseph Smith, the Prophet*, 56–59.

to practice folk-magic of various kinds.[128] In fact, in one instance, Joseph Sr. claimed to have been a firm believer in occult practices and even boasted of having raised his family to believe in such things.[129] In a rather broad sense, "occult practices" simply means the kinds of rituals and practices intended to endow the practitioner with secret, supernatural knowledge or power, and we will continue to use this definition as we move on. While Joseph Sr.'s involvement with occult and magic during the family migration period is somewhat unclear, by the time of the family's arrival in Palmyra, New York, Joseph Sr.'s magical practices were undeniable.[130] They were certainly passed on to his son Joseph.

The Smith family's interest in occult practices and folk-magic was not the norm for most Americans of this period, but it was certainly not unheard of among New Englanders. Throughout the eighteenth and nineteenth centuries, New England was littered with occult practitioners and publications encouraging the use of magic.[131] As will be seen, these interactions with magic among the Smith family provide a greater context for understanding Joseph Smith Jr.'s antipathy toward Nicene Christian orthodoxy. However, to summarize the data presented thus far: by the time the eleven year-old Joseph Smith Jr. arrived in Palmyra, New York, he had been directly influenced by his grandfather Asael's Universalism, Solomon Mack's end-of-life mysticism, both Joseph Sr. and Lucy's aversion to established orthodoxy, their emphasis upon highly personalized religion, and Joseph Sr.'s constant visions and dreams. Moreover, one can safely assume Joseph Jr. was familiar with his uncle Jason Mack's attempts to establish an alternative religious community. So, by the time Joseph Jr. began practicing magic with his father in Palmyra, New York, he had already been exposed to a variety of unorthodox, and in some cases anti-Nicene ideologies.

Joseph Smith in Palmyra, New York

After arriving in Palmyra, New York, the Smith family began to establish itself in the fabric of the local community. Palmyra was a small town with little to make it a place of note other than the fact that it was at the center of

---

128. Bushman, *Joseph Smith: Rough Stone Rolling*, 47.

129. Abanes, *One Nation Under Gods*, 29.

130. Bushman, *Joseph Smith: Rough Stone Rolling*, 46–47.

131. Quinn, *Early Mormonism and the Magic World View*, 16–23.

religious enthusiasm engendered by the Great Awakening.[132] Many of the towns and villages that experienced repeated revivals and became popular stops for travelling evangelists were eventually referred to as "the burned-over district." This designation was due to the way in which religious enthusiasm and revivals had repeatedly suffused that region.[133] Palmyra, New York, was at the epicenter of an increasingly dynamic and religiously diverse region of pre-Civil War, New England.[134] Consequently, this region of the United States became quite replete with new religious movements and self-proclaimed prophets.[135]

Amidst this post-revivalist culture, the Smith men began a business venture that made use of their interest in the occult: money-digging.[136] It is possible that during the Smiths' life in Vermont they became acquainted with using occult sciences and ritual magic for locating buried treasure. Michael Quinn notes that during the 1700s, Vermont was a hot-bed for money-digging activities.[137] Further, Palmyra was one of numerous towns whose young people experienced a great deal of interest in magic and the practice of money-digging. Often, those participating in magical rituals blended folk-level Christian theology with occult practices, thereby creating, in essence, a new and distinct form of "Christianity."[138]

Regardless of the regional interest in money-digging and magical practices, the Smiths (including Joseph Jr.) forged a reputation among their contemporaries for claiming special skill in such activities.[139] While money-digging and occult practices do not necessarily lead one to conclude that Joseph Smith was destined to develop and codify anti-Nicene theology, it certainly establishes that many of his spiritual activities ran counter to Nicene orthopraxy. This information is just one more piece of a larger puzzle that reveals Joseph Smith's theological propensity for that which is outside the bounds of Nicene orthodoxy.

132. Brodie, *No Man Knows My History*, 15.

133. Howe, *What Hath God Wrought*, 173; Remini, Joseph Smith, 31.

134. Foster, "The Burned-Over District," 94–96.

135. Stone, "Nineteenth and Twentieth-Century American Millennialism," 494–495.

136. Remini, *Joseph Smith*, 32; Abanes, *One Nation Under Gods*, 28–29.

137. Quinn, *Early Mormonism and the Magic World View*, 25.

138. Ibid, 27.

139. Caswall, *The Prophet of the Nineteenth Century*, 29–30.

Religious Dissent

The religious landscape of the post-revolutionary era was a fertile ground in which to grow new religious movements.[140] Numerous unorthodox and anti-Nicene sects began to take form in the decades following the American Revolution, and many of the areas in which Joseph Smith and his family resided were known for such activity.[141] As these data will indicate, it is quite possible that these religious dissenters influenced the thought of Joseph Smith.

Religious Dissent: Isaac Bullard

During Joseph Smith's lifetime, a number of unorthodox movements seemed to cross his path or come into close proximity of his dwelling place. For instance, Isaac Bullard's "Pilgrim" movement originated just a short walking distance from the Smith family's residence in Woodstock, Vermont.[142] Admittedly, this movement formalized in the months following the Smith family's move to Palmyra, New York, but the period in which this group began to establish itself is unclear. However, it is probable that this movement was known prior to the Smith family's exodus.

Isaac Bullard's most distinguishing characteristic was his proclivity for avoiding baths, shaving, and his custom of wearing only a bearskin garment.[143] Theologically, Bullard pursued commitments to free-love and communistic practices.[144] Dubbed "Mummyjum" by the Shakers, Isaac Bullard professed himself to be a prophet.[145] While few of Bullard's theological beliefs are known, what can be ascertained is that Bullard preached the imminent end of all things and his appointment by God as the prophet for the end of the world.[146] Perhaps more interesting than the group's rise near the Smith family farm in Woodstock is the fact that Vermont is the migration path on which Bullard took his followers as he led them toward Missouri. Isaac Bullard led his followers on the very same path of migration from

---

140. Fuller, *Religious Revolutionaries*, 69.

141. Newman, *The Real History of the End of the World*, 184.

142. Brodie, *No Man Knows My History*, 12.

143. Ibid.

144. Tucker, *Another Gospel*, 43.

145. Newman, *The Real History of the End of the World*, 210.

146. Ibid.

Vermont as Joseph Smith Jr. would take, including stops throughout Ohio before ending in Missouri.[147]

So, did Isaac Bullard directly influence Joseph Smith? A sound answer is difficult to ascertain without much speculation, although Woodbridge Riley refers to the Pilgrim movement as a prototype for Mormonism.[148] What can be established is that a self-proclaimed prophet arose within walking distance of the Smith family farm in Vermont.[149] This prophet proclaimed that the end of the world was near and that those seeking salvation must follow him and his teaching. Additionally, this same prophet led his followers through New York and Ohio before setting his sights on Missouri, which was also to be the site of Smith's promise land. Although not a direct parallel to the eventual claims of Joseph Smith Jr., the presence of such an individual in close proximity to a young Joseph Smith is notable. At a minimum, insofar as Smith knew of it, it bequeathed him a plan that he could follow, should such a contingency ever occur.

Jemima Wilkinson

As Ruth Tucker writes, the Universal Friends movement, founded by Jemima Wilkinson, established itself not far from Palmyra, New York.[150] Jemima Wilkinson began her career as a prophetess shortly after she supposedly died and experienced subsequent resurrection.[151] Initially, she began practicing faith healing, prophesying, and dream interpretation. By the time Jemima founded her community in New York, she had abandoned faith healing and instead was known for being a self-proclaimed prophetess.[152] Some of the established details of Wilkinson's belief system included her disregard for traditional marriage, which included the fact that she urged her followers to abandon their spouses who did not join the Universal Friends. Furthermore, there is substantial confusion regarding whether or not Wilkinson claimed to be Jesus Christ in female form, something her followers were quick to assert. What is clear is that two other prophets

---

147. Ibid, 210–211; Tucker, *Another Gospel*, 43.

148. Riley, *The Founder of Mormonism*, 45–46.

149. Ibid, 46.

150. Tucker, *Another Gospel*, 42.

151. Ibid; Hudson, *History of Jemima Wilkinson*, 21.

152. Wisbey, *Pioneer Prophetess*, 21.

claiming to be Daniel and Elijah, prophesying in "these latter days," accompanied Wilkinson.[153]

Even though Wilkinson's Universal Friends society was not in Palmyra, New York, nor adjacent to it, this "Jerusalem" was only twenty-five miles from Palmyra. Moreover, it was not uncommon for the Palmyra newspaper to publish articles critical of Wilkinson and the Universal Friends.[154] As with Bullard, Wilkinson's proximity to Joseph Smith does not necessarily mean that she had direct influence upon Smith. However, it is again significant that a movement emphasizing unorthodox teachings, prophecies, and alternative communities was near to and known in Smith's town of Palmyra, New York.

Ann Lee

One of the most popular, alternative religious sects during Joseph Smith's lifetime was that of the Shakers. Following the death of her four children (three during birth and one in early childhood), Ann Lee began to undergo a theological evolution. Having once sat under the preaching of George Whitefield, Ann Lee finally came to the conclusion that all sexual activity was sinful. Consequently, Ann believed that God revealed to her that the sin for which Adam and Eve were found guilty was actually sexual intercourse.[155] After facing relentless persecution in her native England for her beliefs, Ann Lee led a group of her devoted followers across the Atlantic Ocean to establish a new religious community in New York.[156] The eventual location of this new community was New Lebanon, New York, only a day's journey from Palmyra, New York.[157]

Taking on a millennial fervor, the Shakers became convinced that Ann Lee was actually Jesus Christ, now ushering in the millennial kingdom.[158] Following the death of Ann Lee in 1784, the Shakers continued to thrive in New Lebanon, New York.[159] Much of their theology centered on the belief that Ann Lee was Jesus Christ returned in female form, and

153. Tucker, *Another Gospel*, 42–43.

154. Brodie, *No Man Knows My History*, 13.

155. Gutek and Gutek, *Visiting Utopian Communities*, 33.

156. Stein, *Communities of Dissent*, 52.

157. Tucker, *Another Gospel*, 40–41.

158. Gutek and Gutek, *Visiting Utopian Communities*, 33–34.

159. Ibid, 37–38.

that prophets were needed to lead God's people.[160] As previously stated, the existence of such a group near Joseph Smith does not mean that Smith's rise as a self-proclaimed prophet outside the bounds of Nicene orthodoxy was a result of living near the Shakers. Still, the fact remains that Joseph Smith would have been familiar with the Shakers and their attempt to establish an alternative religious society opposed to Nicene orthodoxy. This proposition is confirmed by the inclusion of a reference to the Shakers in the LDS collection of prophetic revelations called Doctrines and Covenants.[161] This revelation, dated to 1831, is meant to deal with the problem of Shakers converting to Mormonism, but still remaining loosely connected to Shaker communities. Thus, by 1831, Joseph Smith not only knew of the Shakers but also was initiating efforts to convert them to Mormonism.

John Humphrey Noyes

Unlike the previous religious leaders mentioned, John Humphrey Noyes (1811–1886) came to prominence following the publication of the Book of Mormon. Yet, Noyes represents a religious dissenter, of the same era as Joseph Smith, who lived in the same region. Therefore, his theology and community are worth evaluating.

In 1831, John Humphrey Noyes was converted to Christianity under revivalist preaching and subsequently enrolled in Andover Theological Seminary.[162] Shortly thereafter, Noyes became disenchanted with Nicene Christianity and turned from orthodoxy to pursue his belief in perfectionism. That is to say, Noyes taught that the long-held Calvinistic doctrine of total depravity, handed down from the Puritans, was incorrect. Instead, according to Noyes, human beings of their own will and exertion could attain a morally perfect state before God.[163]

Noyes further moved beyond the bounds of Nicene orthodoxy by proclaiming that God spoke to him alone.[164] In addition, Noyes rejected the traditional Christian view of monogamous marriage for what he called

---

160. Tucker, *Another Gospel*, 42.

161. D&C 49:1.

162. Stein, *Communities of Dissent*, 62; Tucker, *Another Gospel*, 43.

163. Gutek and Gutek, *Visiting Utopian Communities*, 127–128.

164. Newman, *The Real History of the End of the World*, 183.

complex marriage.[165] This view of marriage mixed polygamy and the generalized sharing of sexual partners among the religious community.[166]

Noyes' community, the Oneida Community, is noteworthy because of the following factors. First, Noyes (1811) and Smith (1805) were born just a few years apart from one another and both Noyes and Smith spent a number of their formative years in Vermont.[167] Second, both men began their ascendency as leaders of new religious communities in New York.[168] Third, both men would eventually espouse complex marriage arrangements.[169] Fourth, both claimed to be the mouthpiece of God.[170] Thus, while John Humphrey Noyes began his move away from Nicene orthodoxy after the publication of the Book of Mormon, the beliefs and history of the Oneida Community demonstrate that Smith's religion bore striking similarities to other alternative religions within the same region and timeframe.

Visionaries

Not all religious dissenters were attempting to initiate new religious movements. Some merely professed for themselves a spiritual or religious experience that must be considered outside the norm of Nicene orthodoxy. A number of the elements undergirding the following experiences would find their way into Joseph Smith's account of his own divine encounter.[171] Many conversion, salvation, and commissioning narratives penned from the late eighteenth century to the middle of the nineteenth century contained explicit claims by the one experiencing the religious epiphany to having seen either angels, God the Father, or Jesus Christ. As former Brigham Young University history professor, Michael Quinn has pointed out, some of these accounts most assuredly were known by Joseph Smith and his family.[172] One such narrative that Quinn believes to be worth mentioning

---

165. Stein, *Communities of Dissent*, 62; Jenkins, *Mystics and Messiahs*, 31–32.

166. Foster, *Religion and Sexuality*, 74.

167. Stein, *Communities of Dissent*, 62.

168. Gutek and Gutek, *Visiting Utopian Communities*, 132; Jenkins, *Mystics and Messiahs*, 31–32.

169. Foster, *Religion and Sexuality*, 74.

170. Newman, *The Real History of the End of the World*, 183.

171. Bushman, *Joseph Smith: Rough Stone Rolling*, 60.

172. Quinn, *Early Mormonism and the Magic World View*, 14.

is that of Richard Brothers.[173] Brothers held a place of prophetic importance while associated with an English prophetess named Joanna Southcott
(1750–1814).[174] Today, Brothers is still held in high regard among a small
prophetic sect referred to as the Jezreelites .[175] According to Brothers, he
was carried to heaven on a cloud where he met God and was given direct,
divine instruction. In Quinn's opinion, it is clear that Smith's family had
access to the various accounts written by Brothers during the 1790's and
distributed throughout Pennsylvania, New York, and Massachusetts.[176]

Another vision bearing similarity to Joseph Smith's own purported
experience is that described by Elias Smith. In 1816, Elias Smith published
an account of a supposed encounter with Jesus Christ. According to Smith,
at the age of sixteen, while walking through the woods, Jesus Christ physically appeared to him.[177] Certainly, the similarity in age to Joseph Smith
when he reportedly experienced his own encounter with Jesus in the flesh,
as well as the woodland setting, is striking. Further adding to the possibility
of potential influence upon Joseph Smith's claims is the fact that Elias Smith
alleged that this event occurred not far from Joseph Smith's own sphere of
dwelling in Woodstock, Vermont.[178]

The account of a vision experienced by Asa Wild was published in the
Palmyra newspaper in 1823. In this account, Asa Wild reported to have
seen God and to have been told that all the churches of the earth were
false.[179] Both of these elements found their way into Joseph Smith's retelling
of his own vision and divine commissioning.

In 1825, while preaching in Palmyra, New York, from January to
March, Universalist minister John Samuel Thompson shared stories of his
own visions. Thompson would report that while living in England he experienced a vision of Jesus Christ returning to earth.[180] For Thompson, this
dream meant that in some sense Jesus had actually returned to earth.

173. Ibid.

174. Allan, "Southcottian Sects from 1790 to the Present Day," 213.

175. Ibid, 214–215.

176. Quinn, *Early Mormonism and the Magic World View*, 14.

177. Smith, *The Life, Conversion, Preaching, Travels, and Sufferings of Elias Smith*, 57–59.

178. Ibid, 48–59.

179. Bushman, *Joseph Smith: Rough Stone Rolling*, 60; Abanes, *One Nation Under Gods*, 21; Quinn, *Early Mormonism and the Magic World View*, 14.

180. Brodie, *No Man Knows My History*, 22; Bushman, *Joseph Smith: Rough Stone Rolling*, 60; Abanes, *One Nation Under Gods*, 21.

Michael Quinn goes on to note that in 1808, a newspaper less than ten miles from Joseph Smith's home featured a front page article regarding Emanuel Swedenborg's supposed encounter with God in the flesh. Further, circulating throughout New York as early as 1805, there were copies of Benjamin Abbott's supposed experience with both Jesus and God the Father. Thus, for Michael Quinn, it was rather commonplace in Joseph Smith's era and region of residence for religious zealots to claim face-to-face experiences with both Jesus Christ and God the Father.[181]

JOSEPH'S VISION

While the specifics of Smith's tritheism will be discussed in chapter 6, it is important to present now the foundation of Smith's theology: his purported experience with Jesus Christ and God the Father. The importance of understanding Smith's First Vision in its historical context cannot be overstated. As the late Mormon president Gordon B. Hinckley (1910–2008) has said, the entirety of the LDS faith stands or falls on the validity of Joseph Smith's First Vision.[182] Given what has been described above regarding religious excitement, potential influences upon Smith, and the Smith family's penchant for unorthodox religion, the details of the First Vision must now be assessed.

The First Vision

In his own account of his First Vision, Joseph Smith states that this event occurred early in the spring of 1820. After a time of religious revival and subsequent soul searching, Smith experienced a sense of spiritual depression. As Smith would claim, he felt the deep desire to be extricated from his spiritual confusion, so he called upon God to impart wisdom to him. Praying out loud for the first time, Smith retired to a wooded area near his home. After reaching a secluded portion of the woods, Smith implored God for guidance regarding which denominations were correct. As Joseph prayed, he recounts, he suddenly lost the ability to speak, and a thick

---

181. Quinn, *Early Mormonism and the Magic World View*, 15.
182. Hinckley, *The Teachings of Gordon B. Hinckley*, 226.

darkness surrounded him. It was then that Smith cried out for deliverance from what he perceived as impending doom.[183]

As Joseph Smith silently cried out for help from God, he claims to have seen a pillar of light descending from heaven. That pillar of light eventually fell upon Joseph Smith. As the pillar of light drove away the darkness, suddenly Smith saw two figures shining brightly and floating in the air above him. According to Smith, these personages were God the Father and God the Son. It was the Father who spoke first, pointing toward the Son, commanding that Joseph hear what the Son had to say.[184]

Joseph claims to have regained his ability to speak and at once asked which of the sects of Christianity were correct, to which the persons responded by declaring that all the creeds of Christendom were corrupt, and their doctrines were false. As Smith reported, he was then commanded not to join with any of these sects of Christendom. Then, after telling Joseph things he could not share with his readers or future audiences, the visions disappeared.[185]

Confusing Details and Accounts of the First Vision

Joseph Smith admitted that his account of the First Vision brought immediate backlash upon him from the clergy in his community.[186] The first official publication of Smith's First Vision appeared in the LDS publication Times and Seasons in 1842. According to Richard Bushman, the first informal account given by Joseph regarding the First Vision saw print in 1832.[187] While Smith's late attestation to his First Vision may not warrant any feelings of disbelief regarding his claims, the rather confusing nature in which the First Vision was initially communicated does demand some caution in accepting Smith's report.

For instance, in the original 1832 account of the First Vision, Smith makes no claim of God the Father commanding him to listen to what the Son has to say.[188] In fact, Richard Abanes states that the early publications of the First Vision in 1832, twice in 1835, 1840, and in 1841 contain a num-

183. Smith, *History of Joseph Smith: The Prophet, by Himself*, 2–5.

184. Ibid, 5.

185. Ibid, 6–7.

186. Ibid, 7.

187. Bushman, *Joseph Smith: Rough Stone Rolling*, 39.

188. Jessee, *The Papers of Joseph Smith: Vol. 1*, 5–7.

ber of contradictory assertions.[189] In the first report (1832) and in the 1841 account, Smith claims to have been fifteen years of age when he had his First Vision.[190] Yet, the versions given twice in 1835 and once in 1840, attest to Smith being fourteen at the time of the vision.[191] Further, the 1832 version has Smith as the one who determines, through Bible study, that all sects of Christianity are incorrect.[192] However, from 1840 onward, all retellings of the First Vision include the assertion that God the Father and God the Son inform Joseph that Christendom had been corrupted. What is more, it was not until the 1842 account of the First Vision that Joseph Smith mentions that his spiritual pursuits were inspired by revivals in and around Palmyra, New York.[193] Although Smith dated these revivals as having occurred in 1819–1820, reports written by Smith and Oliver Cowdery in the Messenger and Advocate date these revivals and the subsequent First Vision to 1823.[194]

What is more interesting, given that the First Vision establishes the basis for Smith's eventual theology, is that the persons whom Smith saw in the First Vision are not definitively identified until the 1840's.[195] In the first few iterations of Smith's story, the persons appearing are identified as the Lord (1832), angels (1835), glorious beings (1840), and heavenly beings (1841).[196] Furthermore, Smith violated the command to avoid aligning himself with any of the sects of Christendom when in 1828 he began attending Methodist Bible studies.[197]

W. Jeffrey Marsh, an LDS adherent, has catalogued the initial ten accounts of the First Vision. Marsh does note many of the differences and nuances in the accounts, but he sees these differences as merely fleshing out the larger narrative rather than raising questions of reliability.[198] In a different manner, Richard Bushman also makes light of the apparent prob-

---

189. Abanes, *One Nation Under Gods*, 16.

190. Jessee, *The Papers of Joseph Smith: Vol. 1*, 402–425.

191. Persuitte, *Joseph Smith and the Origins of the Book of* Mormon, 22–23; Jessee, *The Papers of Joseph Smith: Vol. 2*, 79.

192. Smith, *The Personal Writings of Joseph Smith*, 5.

193. Abanes, *One Nation Under Gods*, 16–17.

194. Cowdery, *Messenger and Advocate*, 42–79.

195. Abanes, *One Nation Under Gods*, 16–17.

196. Jessee, *The Papers of Joseph Smith: Vol. 1*, 5–7; Jessee, *The Papers of Joseph Smith: Vol. 2*, 68–79.

197. Newell and Avery, *Mormon Enigma: Emma Hale Smith*, 25; Tucker, *Origin, Rise and Progress of Mormonism*, 18.

198. Marsh, *The Eyewitness History of the Church*, 84–99.

lems with the First Vision story asserting that Smith most likely did not understand the significance of this event.[199] Moreover, Bushman believes that Smith understood the First Vision in terms of his own conversion event and therefore initially relayed details as they seemed important to his conversion story.[200] Marsh and Bushman's dismissal is difficult to accept when considering the substantive differences existing between the original accounts of the First Vision. As Kathleen Flake has stated, the First Vision stands as the basis of Smith's theology of God, specifically his tritheism.[201] Yet, as the data examined demonstrate, the basis of Smith's theology, the First Vision, is as an account riddled with contradicting versions and ever-changing details.

CONCLUSION

The purpose of the present chapter is to answer the following two research questions: First, what was the historical context in which Joseph Smith formulated his tritheism? Second, in what manner did Joseph Smith's theological environment encourage theological innovation? The data presented answered the first research question by providing a number of important details.

First, the orthodoxy that pervaded the American colonies came under attack from a variety of avenues. The established church, along with its creeds, became viewed by many as aligned with Old World tyrannical rule. The rise of republicanism, and specifically Christian republicanism, gave way to a sense of freedom from established orthodoxy.

Second, the events of the Great Awakening, although promoting orthodoxy, led to a radical shift in understanding religious experience. There arose among the colonies a desire for new and expressive forms of religion that were highly individualized. This further weakened the strength of creedal Christianity as the necessary defender of Nicene orthodoxy.

Third, the ideals of religious freedom that permeated the American Revolution gave impetus to novel, unorthodox religious movements coming to the new American nation. This information provides the groundwork for answering the second research question driving the content of this chapter: In what manner did Joseph Smith's theological environment

199. Bushman, *Joseph Smith and the Beginnings of Mormonism*, 56.
200. Ibid, 61–62.
201. Flake, *The Politics of American Religious Identity*, 117–118.

encourage theological innovation? As discussed, the post-revolution American theological landscape was still largely orthodox, but there was a rapidly growing number of unorthodox factions throughout New England just prior to and during the life of Joseph Smith. His own family either embraced or dabbled in varying forms of anti-Trinitarian religion, mysticism, and occultism. Further, Joseph's own uncle attempted to found and lead an alternative religious community meant to restore ancient Christianity. In some manner, these influences impacted the thought of Joseph Smith.

Additionally, the locales in which the Smiths lived in Vermont and New York were in close proximity to a number of unorthodox teachers and sects. Among these possible influences were Isaac Bullard, Jemima Wilkinson's Universal Friends, and Ana Lee's Shakers. Similarly, in Smith's own context there emerged religious communities that rivaled Mormonism, including the Oneida Community. This setting would certainly seem to provide an environment in which theological innovation and deviation from Nicene orthodoxy was well-established. However, the potential influences upon Smith exceed even these religious movements.

During Smith's formative years, he was exposed to a number of visionaries proclaiming either unorthodox, anti-orthodox, or heterodox concepts. Smith had either direct access to or lived in close proximity to a number of visionaries who proclaimed to have seen God the Father (as Smith later claimed), that the end of the world was near, and that Christendom was corrupt— concepts similar to the ones that made their way into Smith's First Vision story. Furthermore, we saw that the foundation of Joseph Smith's theology (discussed in chapter 6), the First Vision, was disseminated in a number of contradictory forms. Throughout the course of recounting his encounter with God the Father and God the Son, Smith would change, rearrange, add, or omit details depending upon his audience. Thus, the very basis of his tritheism stands on rather suspect ground.

All of this information answered the questions guiding the research for this chapter by establishing that Joseph Smith was born into a time of great religious change. Further, his religious context was one that naturally encouraged individual religious expression and the questioning of historic orthodoxy. Even Smith's family life was one that favored individual vision, revelation, and religious expression over and above orthodox creeds. What is more, Joseph Smith grew up in a region littered with unorthodox or anti-orthodox movements, teachers, and self-proclaimed visionaries. Therefore, the development of Smith's tritheism is rather unsurprising and stands merely as one of many unorthodox and anti-Trinitarian movements of the early nineteenth century, originating in either Vermont or New York.

Chapter 5

Joseph Smith's Tritheism

INTRODUCTION

The previous chapter demonstrated that Joseph Smith's theological environment was one that included a variety of potential and probable influences. Some of the popular theological proclamations of the day appear to have been adapted into the basis of Smith's own theology, the First Vision. It was this First Vision that grounded the entirety of Joseph Smith's theology, including his eventual adoption of tritheism. The purpose of the present chapter is to answer the following research question: What was Smith's doctrine of God, and how has this doctrine been revised or clarified by LDS leadership over nearly two centuries into its modern formulation?

The answer to this question will be arrived at by the following route: First, theological elements of Smith's holy book, the Book of Mormon, will be examined. Second, Smith's own words, as revealed in Doctrines & Covenants will be assessed. Last, notable or major changes in the LDS doctrine of God, since the time of Smith, will be engaged.

SOURCES OF LDS THEOLOGY

Describing in detail the sources from which LDS adherents develop their theology is no easy task. Because Mormons believe in continuing revelation, as well as modern apostles and prophets, ascertaining what is authoritative is somewhat problematic. As Robert Millet has noted, LDS doctrine is a "living" theology that experiences change. This means that what was believed in the past to be official doctrine may no longer be binding.[1] Furthermore, the lack of professional clergy, sanctioned systematic theology texts, and no official catechism renders the fine details of LDS doctrinal parameters a shade of grey rather than black and white.

Additionally, according to LDS apostle D. Todd Christofferson, the pronouncements of a prophet or apostle may or may not be doctrinally binding (*Salt Lake City Tribune*, April 8, 2012). Therefore, holding as closely to what is considered authoritative in some sense is helpful in examining LDS theology.

Generally, the LDS doctrine of God is derived from three types or groups of sources. First, LDS Scripture is authoritative.[2] The corpus of LDS revealed texts include the *Book of Mormon, Doctrine and Covenants,* and that which is collected in *The Pearl of Great Price.* Second, the statements of Joseph Smith recorded throughout Mormon publications, although not officially Scripture, are instructive for LDS adherents and leadership in discerning doctrine.[3] Third, the statements of Mormon leaders, apostles, and prophets carry weight in settling or establishing LDS orthodoxy.[4]

This final source group mentioned for understanding LDS theology includes Brigham Young University scholars who routinely speak out on matters of LDS doctrine. Such consultation is necessary because of the manner in which contemporary leaders interpret LDS doctrine. The contours of Mormon theology are ever-changing and are routinely reshaped.[5] Thus, while certain beliefs and concepts are central to the LDS doctrine of God, the way in which LDS scholars speak of these doctrines today must be grasped in order to have the most current understanding of Mormon tritheism.

1. Millet, "What is Our Doctrine?," 17–19.

2. Blomberg and Robinson, *How Wide the Divide?*, 73–74.

3. Ibid, 57–58.

4. McConkie, *Mormon Doctrine*, 765.

5. Oman, "Jurisprudence and the Problem of Church Doctrine," 1–19.

THE BOOK OF MORMON

The Golden Plates

In the previous chapter, it was noted that published accounts of Smith's First Vision did not appear until after the publication of the Book of Mormon in 1830. Yet, as demonstrated in that chapter, according to Smith, it was his First Vision that began the spiritual journey that would result in being directed to find the Book of Mormon. Following his First Vision experience, as Smith recounts, on the night of September 21, 1823 an angel named Moroni appeared to him.[6] Joseph had spent most of the night awake and praying when Moroni appeared and proclaimed to him that his sins were forgiven. Moreover, Moroni informed Smith that he was being commissioned by God to retrieve and translate an ancient book, inscribed upon golden plates, which provided details concerning the early inhabitants of the New World.[7] This record, as described in the preface to the Book of Mormon, covered a span of time from 600 B.C. to A.D. 421.[8] Furthermore, Smith would be the instrument by which God would restore true doctrine to the world through a renewed church founded upon his life and work.[9]

Moroni continued to appear before Joseph, his visits culminating in the command to locate what would become the Book of Mormon. The location of the plates, upon which the book was inscribed, were in a hill called Cumorah, about three miles from Joseph Smith's home.[10] Smith put forth great effort in trying to locate the golden plates. He found them stored in a stone box, buried deep in the hillside.[11] As Joseph attempted to take the plates from the stone box, Moroni appeared and forbade him because

---

6. Smith, *History of Joseph Smith: The Prophet, by Himself*, 9–11; Bushman, *Joseph Smith: Rough Stone Rolling*, 44; Smith, *Biographical Sketches of Joseph Smith, the Prophet*, 81–86; Givens, *By the Hand of Mormon*, 11; Gutjahr, *The Book of Mormon: A Biography*, 14; Reynolds, *The Story of the Book of Mormon*, 409–410.

7. Smith, *History of Joseph Smith: The Prophet, by Himself*, 9–11; Bushman, *Joseph Smith: Rough Stone Rolling*, 44; Givens, *By the Hand of Mormon*, 11.

8. Givens, *The Book of Mormon: A Very Short Introduction*, 3.

9. Marsh, *The Eyewitness History of the Church*, 49–50; Smith, *History of the Prophet Joseph Smith*, 75; Gutjahr, *The Book of Mormon: A Biography*, 14.

10. Peterson, *Moroni: Ancient Prophet, Modern Messenger*, 92; Reynolds, *The Story of the Book of Mormon*, 407; Givens, *By the Hand of Mormon*, 11.

11. Smith, *History of Joseph Smith: The Prophet, by Himself*, 15–16.

of the greed that filled Joseph's heart upon seeing the gold upon which the writings were etched.[12]

According to Smith, he was told to return one year later to Cumorah, but he again did not take possession of the plates.[13] Joseph reportedly made an annual return to Cumorah across a span of four years, each time failing to gain access to the plates. However, Joseph was finally given the plates by Moroni in September of 1827.[14] Mormon tradition holds that there were four types of metallic records present: the larger and smaller Plates of Nephi, the Plates of Mormon, the Plates of Ether (which reportedly contained textual comments made by Moroni), and the Brass Plates of Laban.[15] While these continued failures to retrieve the plates may seem to be a debacle to some, Mormons have traditionally understood the numerous interactions with Moroni to have been especially valuable in shaping Joseph Smith for his role as prophet.[16] Having been forbidden from showing the plates to anyone, under the threat of destruction, Smith undertook a translation of the plates until they became finalized as the Book of Mormon.[17]

Monotheistic Theology in the Book of Mormon

Throughout the text of the Book of Mormon (1830), there appears to be a consistently monotheistic motif. However, by 1844 Joseph Smith was espousing his belief in a plurality of gods.[18] Therefore, laying aside the issue of Joseph Smith as author rather than translator of the Book of Mormon,[19] the content of the Book of Mormon must be examined prior to assessing the changing statements of Smith as prophet.

Early in the Book of Mormon, a seemingly Trinitarian approach is taken in describing the Godhead. The most explicitly Trinitarian presentation of the Godhead comes in III Nephi 11:27 where the author represents Jesus as saying that the Father, Son, and Holy Spirit all "indwell" one another

---

12. Brodie, *No Man Knows My History*, 40.

13. Smith, *History of Joseph Smith: The Prophet, by Himself*, 16.

14. Ibid, 18.

15. Hardy, *The Book of Mormon: A Reader's Edition*, 656.

16. Marsh, *The Eyewitness History of the Church*, 46.

17. Smith, *History of Joseph Smith: The Prophet, by Himself*, 12–13.

18. Smith, *Teachings of the Prophet Joseph Smith*, 370.

19. For a thorough examination of Smith's role in the writing of the Book of Mormon, see Cowdrey, Davis, and Vanick, *Who Really Wrote the Book of Mormon?*.

and are therefore one God. This statement, which the narrative presents as coming from Jesus Christ, does not lead one to assume Trinitarianism within the Book of Mormon. However, elsewhere in the text, vaguely Trinitarian verbiage abounds. For instance, in 1 Nephi 13:41 the author states that there is only one shepherd over all the earth and that this shepherd is the one God. Similarly, in 2 Nephi 31:21, it is declared that the Father, the Son, and the Holy Spirit are not a plurality of gods but are one God.

In the opinion of Joseph McConkie and Robert Millet, this latter reference is merely denoting the need for unity among LDS believers, as there is unity among the Father, the Son, and the Holy Spirit to act as one God.[20] Likewise, George Reynolds and Janne Sjodahl argue that this passage is meant to convey a notion of unity among the persons of the Godhead, rather than a unity in nature or essence.[21] This interpretation succeeds in maintaining the Mormon belief in a plurality of gods while adopting monotheistic language.

Throughout the Book of Mormon, numerous superficially orthodox descriptions of God are present. For instance, in Alma 11:26–31 the author writes that there is only one God. While the interpretation of "oneness" language such as that put forth by Reynolds and Sjodahl can be proposed, it simply falls short of being a persuasive argument.[22] Certainly, as will be seen, contemporary LDS thinkers[23] interpret the plural persons of the Godhead as one in purpose, but to dismiss this oneness, found repeatedly throughout the Book of Mormon, as mere unity in purpose is less than convincing. The weakness of such an interpretation is that it requires later revelation,[24] not interpretation, to provide a basis for the approach taken by Reynolds and Sjodahl.

Elsewhere in the Book of Mormon, there appears to be a modalistic understanding of God. For instance, in Mosiah 15:1–5, the author writes that at the incarnation, God the Father came to earth as Christ. Upon coming to earth as Christ, He became known as God the Son. Further, once God became the Son, His previous existence became recognized as divine Fatherhood. Essentially, this text presents God as functioning in modes of existence rather than being simultaneously Father, Son, and Spirit. The

---

20. McConkine and Millet, *Doctrinal Commentary on the Book of Mormon*, 365.

21. Reynolds and Sjodahl, *Commentary on the Book of Mormon*, 1909.

22. Ibid.

23. Millet, *A Different Jesus?*, 117.

24. Roberts, *History of the Church: Volume 6*, 476.

author of Mosiah 15:1–5 further notes that this change in roles reveals how one can say that there is one God but a multiplicity of persons.

Moreover, Mosiah 3:5–8 recounts the incarnation of Christ by routinely using Father and Son as designations for the deity coming to earth to dwell among men. Dan Vogel has proposed that these texts, among others, demonstrate that the early Book of Mormon and LDS doctrine as a whole had undeniably modalistic overtones. However, observations of modalism in the Book of Mormon do not undermine LDS doctrine. Because of the rather fluid and evolving nature of LDS revelation, the evolution from modalistic imagery in the Book of Mormon to tritheistic language in the teaching of Joseph Smith is seen as nothing more than progress in revelation.[25]

While LDS commentaries do little in commenting on the passages mentioned or providing in-depth, analytical studies, there is nevertheless a consistent understanding of these passages: the Godhead is one in purpose but not in being. The question then is this: did Joseph Smith initially understand these passages as referring to persons who are one in purpose and not in essence? Smith's own teachings reveal the evolution in his theology.

MONOTHEISM TO TRITHEISM IN LDS PUBLICATIONS

While the Book of Mormon, if authored by Joseph Smith, may be of some value in exploring the doctrinal development of Smith, the most explicit theological statements come from the LDS text Doctrines and Covenants. This collection of sermons and prophetic announcements provides a clear picture of what Smith taught and when he taught it. Again, as in the Book of Mormon, it appears that the early prophetic career of Joseph Smith had some monotheistic elements.

In section twenty of *Doctrine and Covenants*, Joseph Smith states that there is a God who is in heaven and is unchangeable, eternal, and the creator of all things.[26] He goes on to explain that this God is Father, Son, and Holy Ghost; all of which are eternal and without end.[27] At least on the surface, this language seems to be blatantly orthodox and even Nicene in orientation. All the more intriguing is the interpretation provided in the LDS commentary on this section of *Doctrine and Covenants*. The explanation advanced is that Smith intends to convey that there are three persons

---

25. Vogel, "The Earliest Mormon Concept of God," 17–33.

26. *D&C* 20:17.

27. *D&C* 20:28.

in the Godhead who are united in essence.[28] The comments supplied by Smith and Sjodahl are quite confusing when combined with what appears just a few lines below this statement. Commenting further, Smith and Sjodahl state that the scriptural teaching regarding the Godhead does not lead to the conclusion of three persons who are one with regard to their being, as advocated in historic orthodoxy.[29]

In 1830, Smith began "re-translating" the book of Genesis under the title, The Book of Moses. It must be noted that Smith lacked any training in the biblical languages. Therefore, referring to Smith's work as a "translation" is tenuous at best. However, because LDS adherents refer to this text as a translation, that designation will be maintained throughout our examination.

Portions of this translation would eventually be incorporated in the Pearl of Great Price. Notably, in this early translation, Smith translates references to God in the singular at least fifty times in chapters 2 and 3 of The Book of Moses. However, it seems that his view of God took an explicitly plural turn at some point between 1832 and 1833. It was during this period that Smith began teaching that human beings themselves can become gods.[30] On the surface, this change in teaching appears to be significant. Regardless, Joseph Smith asserted that a plurality of gods had always been at the foundation of his theology and public teaching.[31] Moreover, Smith went on to profess that human beings have always existed, in some undefined sense, at least in spirit form, alongside of God and are therefore uncreated.[32]

The traditional LDS interpretation is that Jesus is the chief spirit child of Elohim and that Jesus (along with the other spirit children) has eternally pre-existed with Elohim, awaiting a body in which to dwell.[33] These data reveal that by 1833 Smith's initially heterodox understanding of the Godhead began to descend into radically unorthodox categories far outside the bounds of Nicene orthodoxy.[34] By 1838, Smith was declaiming that Mormons worship Elohim as the highest God above the council of gods.[35]

---

28. Smith and Sjodahl, Doctrine and Covenants Commentary, 108.

29. Ibid.

30. D&C 76:50–60

31. Roberts, History of the Church: Volume 6, 474.

32. D&C 93:29

33. Smith and Sjodahl, Doctrine and Covenants Commentary, 123.

34. Kirkland, "The Development of the Mormon Doctrine of God," 36.

35. D&C 121:32

Therefore, even though many gods do exist, Smith exhorted LDS adherents to worship Elohim as the supreme God for this world.

Given this change in theological direction and along with the content of Smith's First Vision experience as it was established subsequently, it would appear to be a natural progression to teach that God the Father and God the Son are not spirits but are instead flesh and bone.[36] Consequently, by 1843, the date of this teaching, Smith had developed a full-fledged notion of plurality not just in persons but a plurality of beings in the Godhead. This proposition is further confirmed by Smith's 1842 translation of the *Book of Abraham*, which is found alongside *The Book of Moses* within the *Pearl of Great Price*. Beginning in the fourth chapter, Smith's translation ceases to speak of a singular God and instead uses the designation "gods." In fact, in chapters 4 and 5, Smith's translation refers to the God of Abraham as "gods" no less than forty-eight times.

While it could be argued that Smith was merely translating the *Book of Abraham* and was therefore not responsible for its substituting "gods" in place of "God," Joseph Smith's 1844 statement regarding the Godhead leaves no room for ambiguity. In 1844, Smith explained that he had always believed in three distinct persons in the Godhead and that these persons are actually "three Gods."[37] When this pronouncement is taken in connection with an article issued in 1844 in the LDS publication *Times and Seasons*, Joseph Smith's vision of tritheism becomes abundantly clear. In *Times and Seasons*, Smith writes that Elohim is now the highest God of our universe, but this was not always the case. Instead, Elohim became God much like LDS followers can also become gods.[38] In the *Journal of Discourse*, Smith is recorded as explaining that God the Father once dwelled on earth in the same manner as Jesus Christ.[39]

In essence, Smith established outright polytheism as a system of thought, but he adhered to tritheism in application. The gods who reign over this present world come from an eternal progression of beings who also became gods in the same manner that LDS adherents strive to attain. In actuality, it was during this period of time that Joseph Smith himself

---

36. *D&C* 130:22

37. Roberts, *History of the Church: Volume 6*, 474.

38. 55. Smith, *Times and Seasons*, 613–614.; Smith, *Teachings of the Prophet Joseph Smith*, 349.

39. Smith, *Journal of Discourse: Volume 6*, 3–4.

admitted that he developed his belief in an eternal regression of gods.[40] Therefore, even though elements of Joseph Smith's move from orthodoxy and into tritheism could be identified throughout his career, his embracing of tritheism had come to full fruition by the early 1840's.[41]

TRITHEISM AFTER JOSEPH SMITH

The Nineteenth Century

Since the death of Joseph Smith, LDS leaders and thinkers have clarified doctrinal teachings regarding the Godhead. In the early decades following the reign of Joseph Smith as prophet, Brigham Young (1801–1877) began to expand upon the doctrinal foundation laid by Joseph Smith. In 1859, Brigham Young explained that there have always been gods, and that the number of these gods is unknown.[42] Yet, what is known is that God the Father was once a man who, through right action, became exalted to the position of God.

In addition, according to Young, LDS adherents can also attain this type of deified position among the gods.[43] This doctrinal assertion was echoed by two early LDS apostles, Parley Pratt (1807–1857) and Orson Hyde (1805–1878). Pratt explained that because of their progression into godhood from their previous positions as mortal men, God the Father and God the Son both possess bodies of flesh and bone.[44] Similarly, in 1853, Orson Hyde stated that God was once a mortal man who grew from childhood to adulthood, ever advancing toward his eventual position as deity.[45] These pronouncements demonstrate that from 1844 to 1859, the idea that Elohim is merely a high God above many other gods was well established among LDS leadership. Moreover, Smith's vision of an infinite regression of gods as former men who attained a deified state, but remained as flesh and bone, was at this point well accepted among LDS leadership.

---

40. Roberts, *History of the Church: Volume 6*, 476.
41. Hale, "Defining the Contemporary Mormon Concept of God," 8.
42. Young, *Journal of Discourses: Volume 7*, 333–334.
43. Ibid, 23.
44. Pratt, *Key to the Science of Theology*, 33–44.
45. Hyde, *Journal of Discourses: Volume 1*, 124.

The Twentieth Century

As time progressed in the post-Joseph Smith LDS world, the descriptions of the Godhead expanded at some points and streamlined at others. In the present, it has become standard practice for leading Brigham Young University professors to utilize historical Nicene terminology, but to infuse that language with LDS meaning. The following examples represent some of the major reaffirmations and even reformulations of Joseph Smith's tritheism.

James Talmage

In 1916, LDS apostle James Talmage (1862–1933) wrote that Elohim and Jehovah are two separate and distinct gods.[46] According to Talmage, the teachings of Joseph Smith and the LDS church as a whole lead to the conclusion that Elohim is the highest God, as God the Father, and Jehovah is a lesser God identified with Jesus Christ. Likewise, Talmage explained that in looking at all three persons of the Godhead, one must understand them as three gods who are one God in unity and purpose.[47]

Additionally, Talmage denounced the orthodox position on the doctrine of the Trinity as utterly inconsistent.[48] It was Talmage's contention that the three persons of the Godhead are not persons as understood by Nicene orthodoxy.[49] Instead, they are three distinct beings (materially), as distinct from one another as any other individual human being. Thus, for Talmage, the only way to consistently interpret the text of Scripture is to adhere to the tritheism of the LDS church.

Bruce McConkie

In the 1970's, LDS apostle Bruce McConkie (1915–1985) wrote that there are an infinite number of gods. These gods progressed from a former state on other "worlds" into exaltation as gods.[50] As McConkie explains, the God of this world or universe, Elohim, must have progressed to His position as

46. Talmage, *Jesus the Christ*, 466–467.
47. Talmage, *The Articles of Faith*, 13.
48. Ibid, 48.
49. Ibid, 37–39.
50. McConkie, *Mormon Doctrine*, 576–577.

deity on a previous world as well.[51] According to McConkie, the Father, Son, and Spirit are distinct and individual gods.[52] Although there are an infinite number of gods in existence, from the LDS perspective, the three gods of the Godhead are the only beings that can be rightly worshiped.[53] Moreover, McConkie asserts that there can be no salvation for those who worship a God who is a "spirit essence" lacking a body or parts.[54] This last statement is meant to contrast Nicene theology with that of Mormonism.

Robert Millet

Most recently, LDS thinkers have begun to actively engage with Nicene Christians on issues relating to the nature of the Godhead. These exchanges provide valuable insights into the current theological trends among LDS leaders in explaining their view of the Godhead. For instance, LDS scholar Robert Millet (1947–) has written a book entitled *A Different Jesus?*, in which he compares the traditional Mormon view of Jesus with that of Nicene Christianity. While attempting to build bridges of communication with Nicene Christians, Millet admits that LDS doctrine envisions multiple gods, one of whom is Jesus, who as a mortal has achieved exaltation as a deity.[55]

Furthermore, God the Father, according to Millet, attained His deified state following His own death and resurrection on another world.[56] Millet explains that the means by which God the Father acquired the attributes associated with deity occurred through a process that encompassed a long, albeit undefined, period of time.[57] This description is interesting given Millet's claim that LDS adherents do, in fact, accept the doctrine of the Trinity. However, Millet is quick to add the caveat that Mormons believe in the doctrine of the Trinity but not in the creedal doctrine clarified in the early church.[58]

51. Ibid, 321.
52. Ibid, 317,
53. Ibid, 163.
54. McConkie, The Caravan Moves On," 82.
55. Millet, *A Different Jesus?*, 20.
56. Millet, *The Mormon Faith*, 29–30.
57. Millet and Reynolds, *Latter-day Christianity*, 32–33.
58. Millet and McDermott, *Claiming Christ*, 78.

It is Millet's opinion that reading the content of Christian Scripture, along with the use of sound reasoning, does not and could not lead to the Nicene understanding of the Trinity.[59] In fact, Millet sees no basis at all for postulating the Nicene position on the doctrine of the Trinity.[60] In a rather telling statement Millet concludes that if agreeing with Nicene orthodoxy is necessary to describe one as a Christian then, based upon the Nicene definition of the Trinity, Mormons could not be considered Christians.[61]

Denying that LDS adherents are polytheistic, Millet argues that Mormons hold to a belief in one God, but that this God is a community of divine beings acting together.[62] To put it another way, Mormons worship a single group of gods acting as one God.[63] Millet's Brigham Young University colleagues Daniel Peterson and Stephen Ricks corroborate this interpretation when they state that to refer to the LDS doctrine of God as tritheism would be accurate.[64] Considering that Millet at one point acknowledges that the LDS Godhead is comprised of three gods, Millet's desire to avoid the term "tritheism" by opting to use the word "Trinity" seems disingenuous.[65] Thus, while taking a more nuanced approach to tritheism than early LDS leaders, Millet still affirms the central tenets of Joseph Smith's tritheism.

Stephen Robinson

Another notable contemporary Mormon theologian is Brigham Young University professor Stephen Robinson (1947–). In his book, *Are Mormons Christian?*, Robinson goes straight to the heart of the issue when he states that Mormons reject Nicene orthodoxy for three reasons. First, LDS adherents believe Nicene Trinitarianism to be unbiblical. Second, the linguistic categories necessary for describing the doctrine of the Trinity are not found within the text of Christian Scripture. Last, Nicene Trinitarianism utilizes elements of Greek philosophy, which Robinson sees as incompatible with a revelatory approach to theology.[66]

---

59. Ibid, 79–80.
60. Millet, *The Mormon Faith*, 188.
61. Millet, *A Different Jesus?*, 171.
62. Millet and McDermott, *Claiming Christ*, 80–81; Millet, *The Mormon Faith*, 28.
63. Millet, *A Different Jesus?*, 117.
64. Peterson and Ricks, "Comparing LDS Beliefs with First-Century Christianity," 67.
65. Millet, *A Different Jesus?*, 141.
66. Robinson, *Are Mormons Christians?*, 72.

Further explaining the LDS position on the Godhead, Robinson asserts that Mormons believe that God the Father and God the Son both have material bodies. Additionally, Robinson explains that this belief is based solely upon the experience of Joseph Smith. He clarifies that this doctrine necessarily has to come from Smith because there is no basis for such a belief in Christian Scripture.[67] In distinction to Robinson's position, LDS scholar Robert Millet argues that this belief, the material nature of the Godhead, is found within the text of Christian Scripture.[68]

Regardless of the difference in opinion between Robinson and Millet, the doctrine of a corporeal Godhead is why Mormons have traditionally understood the biblical statement that God made mankind in His image (Gen. 1:26–28) to mean His own physical image.[69] Because humans are like God, Stephen Robinson argues, they can eventually become more like God in reaching a deified position.[70] Simply put, the LDS doctrine is that humans are divine in nature and species.[71] Consequently, human beings, in a sense, are non-actualized gods.

In the course of addressing Nicene Trinitarianism, Robinson elucidates his own understanding of LDS doctrine. According to Robinson, LDS adherents readily affirm the Nicene formulation "one God in three persons"; however, Mormons reject the notion that this oneness has anything to do with ontology or essence. Instead, the LDS approach is to envision three distinct beings who are merely one in purpose, mind, and intentions.[72] For Robinson, the doctrine of the Trinity is not a problem for Mormons; the issue arises when the "one God" of Nicaea is defined as one being and not just one God in purpose.[73]

In explicating the LDS position on three gods acting as one God, Robinson writes that these gods are not "absolute being" as classical definitions of God would imply. Instead, these beings are each contingent in some sense. Robinson rationalizes this differentiation from classical formulations

---

67. Blomberg and Robinson, *How Wide the Divide?*, 78.

68. Millet, *The Mormon Faith*, 188.

69. Robinson, *Are Mormons Christians?*, 80.

70. Blomberg and Robinson, *How Wide the Divide?*, 80.

71. Ibid, 82–86.

72. Ibid, 129.

73. Robinson, *Are Mormons Christians?*, 71.

by claiming that classical definitions cannot be sustained from the Christian Scripture, but only from Greek philosophy.[74]

Going further, Robinson asserts that LDS adherents are absolutely committed to subordinationism. Therefore, Robinson's statement that Mormons could be called Trinitarians, but not in the sense intended by the Nicene tradition, is rather misleading because it veils LDS tritheism in orthodox-sounding language.[75] So, in the case of Robinson, there is a clear attempt to employ Nicene language while applying LDS definitions. Rather than enabling communication between Mormons and Nicene Christians, this borrowing from the Nicene lexicon seems to lead to a greater level of confusion.

Summary

Throughout the history of the LDS church, Mormon prophets, apostles, and scholars have sought to clarify, explain, and expound the doctrine of God as put forth by Joseph Smith. These discussions have been successful in reaffirming central elements of Joseph Smith's theology. The core tenets are as follows: First, there are many gods, but Mormons worship one group of three gods who act as a single God. Second, these gods progressed to their state as deities from a previously mortal condition. This means then that there is an eternal progression and regression of mortal beings who are now gods.[76] Third, Mormons seek to correct the Nicene understanding of the Trinity by supplanting it with the tritheism of Joseph Smith. In the course of these corrections, Mormons leaders and scholars make use of Nicene terminology that has been infused with LDS meanings. Therefore, pointing out the necessary distinctions between LDS doctrine and Nicene orthodoxy has become fundamentally important.

THE GREAT APOSTASY

According to LDS authoritative works, shortly after the apostolic age, a "Great Apostasy" occurred, and the Christian church became corrupt. As a result, the doctrines clarified in the early church are null and void

---

74. Ibid, 68.

75. Blomberg and Robinson, *How Wide the Divide?*, 130–131.

76. White, *Mormon Neo-Orthodoxy*, 59–62.

because they come out of a church that is inherently false. This attitude arises directly from the text of the Book of Mormon. The author of 1 Nephi writes that all the churches of Christendom became corrupted and are an abomination to God (1 Nephi 13:5–6).

In *Doctrines and Covenants*, it is recorded that Joseph Smith called the Protestant church the "whore of the earth," declaring that this abominable institution will be thrown down.[77] Moreover, LDS adherents are taught that Joseph Smith did not introduce the most correct form of Christianity to the world; rather, Smith introduced a restored and corrected form of Christianity meant to replace Nicene Christianity. Therefore, the LDS adoption of tritheism is seen as a restoration of apostolic doctrine rather than a fundamentally new religion.

The LDS justification for professing to believe that true doctrine had been abandoned in the early church is primarily based upon a prophecy Amos 8:11–12. The text in question reads:

> "Behold, the days are coming," declares the Lord God" when I will send a famine on the land—not a famine of bread, nor a thirst for water, but of hearing the words of the Lord.
>
> They shall wander from sea to sea, and from north to east; they shall run to and fro, to seek the word of the Lord, but they shall not find it." (ESV)

According to LDS luminaries, this prophetic utterance predicted that there will come a time when the doctrine of the Apostles is lost and there would be no true church found anywhere.[78] As Bruce McConkie commented, following the life of the Apostle John, there was a total and complete falling away from true doctrine that lasted until the time of Joseph Smith.[79] The LDS First Presidency publication, *True to the Faith*, explains that while churches have been established throughout history since the time of the apostasy, the true church did not return until the time of Smith's First Vision.[80] To summarize Parley Pratt's opinion of this period, the church ceased to exist after the death of the Apostles, and what remained was a perversion of true (LDS) doctrine.[81]

77. *D&C* 29:21

78. Talmage, *The Great Apostasy*, 26.

79. McConkie, *Mormon Doctrine*, 529.

80. The First Presidency, *True to the Faith*, 13.

81. Pratt, *Key to the Science of Theology*, 67–68.

The LDS method for avoiding the accusation that tritheism is a new and innovative doctrine introduced by Joseph Smith is to posit an early corruption of all Christian doctrine. By implication, Nicene orthodoxy is merely the culmination of pagan ideals infiltrating originally pure, Christian doctrine. In light of the data presented in chapter 3, it would be difficult to propose that Trinitarian concepts were foreign in the early church. However, in order for Smith's doctrine to be a viable alternative to Nicene orthodoxy, LDS apologists must propose that it came prior to Trinitarianism.

ASSESSING JOSEPH SMITH'S TRITHEISM

The rationale for adhering to Nicene orthodoxy, based upon the text of Christian Scripture, was thoroughly argued in chapter 3. While the present chapter will not seek to repeat all of the data previously discussed, the reader is invited to hold the theological claims of Joseph Smith against the case presented in the aforementioned chapter. Additionally, we will recall issues such as the Great Apostasy and the historical progress of Nicene orthodoxy found in chapter 3. Without fundamentally repeating the same information, pertinent details from chapter 4 will be referenced to when necessary.

The Evolution of Smith's Theology

The proposition that Smith's theology evolved from one that was either heterodox or superficially orthodox fits the extant data. Even though Smith professed to have experienced his First Vision in 1820, the details of that First Vision did not become public and widely known until 1832.[82] As previously mentioned, the Book of Mormon was first published in 1830. This means, as of 1830, the only published LDS Scripture contained numerous references to the Godhead that seemed to teeter between orthodoxy and modalism.

The proposal that during this period Smith was at least comfortable with Nicene Christianity makes sense, in light of the fact that as late as 1828

---

82. Smith, *History of Joseph Smith: The Prophet, by Himself*, 5; Bushman, *Joseph Smith: Rough Stone Rolling*, 39.

Joseph was actively participating in Methodist Bible studies.[83] In 1830, Smith was still publicly using Nicene language to describe the Godhead as a single, eternal, and unchangeable God.[84] Furthermore, in an attempt to correct the book of Genesis, Smith produced a translation that through the first three chapters contains references to God in the singular no less than fifty times (Moses 1:1–3:25).

In the mid-to-late 1830's, Joseph Smith began espousing an explicit belief in a plurality of gods.[85] By the time of his 1842 translation of the *Book of Abraham*, Smith's theology was undeniably anti-Trinitarian.[86] As previously noted, in the fourth and fifth chapter of the *Book of Abraham*, Smith refers to the Godhead as "gods" forty-eight times. In 1844, following the publication of the *Book of Abraham*, Smith repeatedly spoke of and wrote about there being a plurality of gods in the universe and specifically within the Godhead.[87] Thus, the publication of the *Book of Abraham*, while not inaugurating Smith's adoption of tritheism, represented the scriptural support necessary for Smith's teaching regarding a multiplicity of gods. As a result, the basis of his translation has to be examined.

In 1835, Smith acquired the scroll from which he translated the *Book of Abraham*. This document was obtained from a traveling Egyptian artifacts exhibit that passed through Kirtland, Ohio.[88] Tragically, it was long believed that the document from which Smith based his explication of the *Book of Abraham* had been destroyed in the Chicago fire of 1871. However, in 1967, while visiting the Metropolitan Museum of Art in New York, University of Utah professor Aziz Atiya discovered much of the original material that Joseph Smith used for his translation of the *Book of Abraham*.[89] Shortly after the discovery of the papyri segments, a translation of the documents was undertaken and found that the text was little more than a common Egyptian funerary description.[90] In fact, the content of the pa-

83. Newell and Avery, *Mormon Enigma: Emma Hale Smith*, 25; Tucker, *Origin, Rise and Progress of Mormonism*, 18.

84. *D&C* 20:17

85. *D&C* 121:32

86. Roberts, *History of the Church: Volume 6*, 474.

87. Smith, *Journal of Discourse: Volume 6*, 3–4; Smith, *Teachings of the Prophet Joseph Smith*, 345–349.

88. Peterson, *Moroni: Ancient Prophet, Modern Messenger*, 1.

89. Fletcher, *A Study Guide to the Facsimiles of the Book of Abraham*, xi; Tucker, *Another Gospel*, 61.

90. Baer, "The Breathing Permit of Hor," 111.

pyri proved to be sections of the Egyptian Book of Breathings and the Book of the Dead.

The stories found in each of the extant facsimiles describe the following: Facsimile one, featuring Osiris and Horus, is a representation of the Egyptian understanding of progress into the afterlife.[91]The second facsimile describes the process by which Osiris Sheshonk's soul will relocate and live on in the afterlife.[92] The third facsimile once again refers to Osiris and Horus, but also includes references to other Egyptians gods: Maat and Anubis.[93] Surprisingly, LDS scholar Hugh Nibley validated these translations in his own work on the facsimiles, while at the same time arguing that there must be other papyri that undergird the content of the *Book of Abraham*.[94] Although this proposition is less than persuasive, it is a necessary adjustment for accepting the *Book of Abraham* if the LDS church is to uphold its position as Scripture. Outside of the revelations given directly to Joseph Smith, the content of the *Book of Abraham* is the major scriptural basis for subscribing to a plurality of gods. In light of the fact that the *Book of Abraham* has been demonstrated to be based upon Smith's faulty translation of Egyptian funerary texts littered with references to Egyptian gods, it seems not only plausible, but also quite likely that Smith's tritheism originated from the bounds of his own imagination.

Joseph Smith's Tritheism: A Definition

Based upon Joseph Smith's varying, often vague, and somewhat contradictory statements on the nature of the Godhead, it can be difficult to ascertain how Smith understood his own tritheism as it might appear in a coherent creed, as it were. If one pieces together statements made by Smith regarding the nature of the Godhead, the following can be established. First, Smith informs his followers that he believes there to be a high God (*Elohim*) who rules over a council of gods.[95] These gods are former human beings who progressed to godhood by adhering to and following Mormon doctrine

91. Ibid, 116–118.

92. Rhodes, "A Translation and Commentary of the Joseph Smith Hypocephalus," 265.

93. Baer, "The Breathing Permit of Hor," 126–127.

94. See Nibley, *The Message of the Joseph Smith Papyri*.

95. *D&C* 121:32

and law.[96] Second, these gods (including *Elohim*) have retained their bodies of flesh and bone.[97] Third, for this world, a plurality of three gods exists and God the Father (*Elohim*) reigns as the highest among these three gods. Fourth, these three gods act as one God and should be worshipped as one God.[98] This last point is the primary means on which LDS adherents rely to explain the explicitly monotheistic language used by Smith throughout his personal journals, many of his sermons, and even in his translations of LDS sacred texts. Arising naturally from this definition of Smith's tritheism, is a variety of questions regarding the theological viability of Joseph Smith's proposals. As a result, we must assess the theological consistency of Joseph Smith's tritheism.

Joseph Smith's Tritheism: A Theological Assessment

One of the primary considerations in engaging Joseph Smith's underdeveloped tritheism is the assumptions one must make in believing that three divine beings (gods) can act together as one divine being (God). Historically speaking, orthodox descriptions of the Godhead (see chapter 3) have denied that the persons of the Godhead are unified merely in the shared intentions of their mutually exclusive wills. Instead, the unity of the persons is genuine and substantial. This genuine, substantial unity could be described through a variety of avenues, but for the purpose of the present research will be explored in three ways. First, the nature of God will be considered as it relates to problems arising by adhering to tritheism. Second, the necessity of divine *perichoresis* shall be considered. Third, the deficiencies inherent to tritheistic worship will be noted.

To state that God is simple is to speak of His absolute unity. A Trinitarian understanding of the Godhead is that God is not composed of parts but is absolute unity.[99] In part, this belief flows naturally from the Scriptural doctrine of divine immutability (Mal. 3:6; Heb. 1:12; Jm. 1:17). Immutability is meant to convey the notion that God's nature does not undergo changes.[100] This is an element of orthodox doctrine that Smith briefly af-

---

96. *D&C* 76:50–60

97. *D&C* 130:22

98. Roberts, *History of the Church: Volume 6*, 474.

99. Shedd, *Dogmatic Theology*, 276–277.

100. Ibid, 284–285; Geisler, *Systematic Theology, Volume 2*, 43; Bray, *God is Love*, 149–153.

firms.[101] Therefore, each of the divine persons of the Trinity do not begin their existence as deity and then engage in sharing in the divine nature; instead, each of the persons of the Godhead have always shared equally in the divine nature or essence.

Considering the range of divine attributes exercised by God through-out the text of Scripture, it can be difficult to imagine the divine nature as being simple. However, even in the created order, it can be seen that a single, unified object exhibits a multiplicity of attributes. For instance, a stone can be described as hard and round. These are two distinct attributes that each accurately describe the same object. It is not logically necessary to have multiple objects in mind when speaking of multiple attributes. Herman Bavinck has expressed this proposition by affirming that God is identical with His attributes and His attributes are identical with His essence.[102] To deny as much, according to Bavinck, is to posit a divine essence that can be shared by a multiplicity of beings. This would mean that attributes of God such as love, power, and majesty can be diminished or increased based upon the levels to which a deity is actively engaged in the use of the divine nature.[103] Bavinck's argument represents a consistent and accurate criticism of Smith's belief that faithful LDS males can become gods.[104] These potential gods, according to Smith, would be part of a hierarchy of gods based upon their attributes.[105]

Moreover, absolute unity does not negate plurality or complexity. This fact is revealed within the created order. For Timothy Tennent, complex and absolute unity can be seen in creation, and he communicates it accurately in the following illustration: A tiger is a creature that is both complex and an instance of absolute unity. While being internally differentiated, the tiger has a singular, unified essence. To state it succinctly, while complex, the tiger is indivisible. Any attempt to divide the tiger in accordance with its plurality or complexity would actually destroy the tiger rather than creating two separate tigers.[106] This illustration demonstrates that complexity and absolute unity in being or essence are not mutually exclusive propositions. The weakness of this illustration is that it attempts to utilise a mate-

---

101. *D&C* 20:17

102. Bavinck, *Reformed Dogmatics*, 175.

103. Ibid, 175–176.

104. *D&C* 76:50–60

105. *D&C* 121

106. Tennent, *Christianity at the Religious Roundtable*, 158.

rial being to illustrate a divine, immaterial reality. This kind of illustration runs counter to the essential nature of Trinitarian theology. However, it is a useful illustration for the purpose of engaging LDS theology, precisely because of Joseph Smith's teachings on the material nature of the divine persons. One way in which orthodox, Nicene Christians have attempted to explain this plural unity in theologically consistent terms is via the concept of *perichoresis*.

Within orthodox Christianity, the term *perichoresis* is used to communicate the notion that the three divine persons (who are simple in being) necessarily contain one another.[107] This doctrine is what constitutes one of the primary, substantive differences between Trinitarianism and Joseph Smith's tritheism. *Perichoresis* is inextricably linked with divine simplicity. Letham quite persuasively argues that the concept of a simple divine essence/nature, shared among three divine persons that co-inhabit one another, speaks to the necessity of no more than three divine persons. As Letham correctly notes, to diminish the co-inhabiting of the divine persons posits distinctions similar to those among human persons. While human persons share in the nature inherent to being human, this is radically different from Trinitarianism and the sharing of the divine nature among the persons of the Trinity. Specifically, the sheer number of human persons sharing in human nature fluctuates based upon worldwide population and each human person is also a separate being. Conversely, within Nicene thought, the number of divine persons remains eternally the same, while there is only one being.[108] If the number of divine persons does not remain constant, then the presence of the divine nature and the execution of attributes inherent to the divine nature would never be consistent.

In the case of Joseph Smith's tritheism, three persons, who are separate beings, have attained access to the divine nature and are to be worshipped as one God by those occupying this world. Interestingly, one of the theological shortcomings of Smith's tritheism is that, while only these three gods are to be worshipped by faithful LDS adherents, an ever-increasing number of beings are reaching the state of enjoying divine nature themselves.[109] This last point is the prime example of the inconsistency of tritheism. This inconsistency can be stated quite simply: the gods of tritheism are beings who either are or have been in need of support for their existence.

---

107. Letham, *The Holy Trinity*, 178.

108. Ibid; Cf. Torrance, *Trinitarian Perspectives*, 35–36.

109. *D&C* 76:50–60

One can argue that, due to the material nature of these three gods, they are perpetually in a state of need because their mere existence depends upon the continued existence of matter. However, the point at-hand is that in the distant past, or presently, they would not have possessed a divine nature. Based upon the hierarchy mentioned by Smith, these gods continue to vary in their ability to access or exercises divine attributes and are, as a result, in need. The dependent nature of these divine beings is further exemplified in Joseph Smith's description of the regression of eternal gods.[110]That is to say that each of these gods would inescapably be dependent upon the existence and progress of previous beings for both their own deity and their sheer existence.

This last point brings up another issue of theological significance: divine necessity. While difficulties pertaining to the logical contradictions of an eternal regression of gods will be examined later, arguments for divine necessity also provide theological insight on these matters. The doctrine of divine necessity is derived from the philosophical reality that all that exists has a cause for its existence. Thomas Aquinas is the most well-known proponent of this argumentation as it relates to the nature of God. According to Aquinas, the divine nature is the necessary being, and this is evident from the natural world and philosophical inquiry.[111] John Frame agrees with the theological proposition that Aquinas presents; however, he views divine necessity as flowing naturally from the text of Scripture rather than being equally from philosophy.[112] Regardless of one's starting point, be it Scripture or philosophy, the logical nature of the assertion made by Aquinas is evident. First, everything known to exist has a cause. Second, there could not be an infinite number of causes spanning an infinite number of past events, because such a scenario would render the present impossible. Thus, there must be one uncaused, necessary being. That being, according to Aquinas is the divine essence/nature shared among the persons of the Trinity.[113] The gods described by Smith's tritheism are not necessary beings but are entirely contingent and dependent upon previous causes for their own existence.

Moreover, Joseph Smith's admonition that LDS adherents should worship these three gods as a single God is rather unintelligible. If these three

---

110. *D&C* 76:50–60

111. Aquinas, *Summa Theologica: Volume 1 Article 1.*

112. Frame, *The Doctrine of God,* 224.

113. Aquinas, *Summa Theologica: Volume 1, Part 1,* 229–230.

beings were equal in every fashion, then such a command would be logical. However, if the beings are each equal in every capacity, then differentiation among the beings would not exist in terms of their deity, but instead in their personhood and relationships. If this were the case, then Smith's tritheism would actually be a poorly developed explanation of Trinitarianism. Still, the difficulty of divine differentiation remains: how can faithful Mormons worship these three gods as one God when each of the beings does not share equally in the divine nature? Each of the beings possesses differing attributes that are supposed to be inherent to deity, and each is progressing further and further into their godhood. As a result, it seems theologically untenable to worship three beings of varying states of godhood as one God. The three beings of tritheism would each be distinguishable from another not just in relationship and role but also in how much worship and adoration they deserve based upon their particular share of the divine nature.

Even more difficult to comprehend theologically is the problem of worship and a unified will. Joseph Smith's explanation for worshipping the three gods as one is based on their actions as one God grounded solely in their unified will. To state it another way, because each of these gods voluntarily chooses to direct the efforts of his will toward the same end as the other two divine beings, their individual wills are unified as one will. The implications for this description are substantial. When LDS adherents, following Smith's leading, worship the three gods as one God, they are actually directing their worship to the unified will of the three beings. Within the bounds of Smith's tritheism, the only unifying aspect of the three divine persons is the unified desires and efforts of their individual wills. Therefore, the aspect of these beings and their relationships that can be remotely described as "one God" would be nothing more than the oneness found in their unified will. Thus, any effort to worship these beings as one God is merely adoration of the unified will of the beings, not deity as deity.

Historic, Nicene Trinitarianism pursues a different and theologically satisfying approach to the nature of God. As described previously, orthodox Christianity proposes that God's nature is simple or indivisible. However, this doctrine does not negate the fact that He is plural in persons. As William Lane Craig and J.P. Moreland have argued, plurality in persons is philosophically and theologically sound insofar as one assumes that triunity is intrinsic to the divine nature or essence.[114] This argument proposes

---

114. Craig and Moreland, *Philosophical Foundations for a Christian Worldview*, 590–591.

that the three divine persons of the Trinity would not exist without one another. Thus, while the Father can rightly be called God, this is not an absolute statement of identity, because the Father is not God alone but is deity insofar as He is the Father of God the Son. The weakness of this argument is that it can be construed in such a manner as to imply that the persons of the Trinity are substantive parts of the Trinity. That is to say that the Triune God is composed of beings in a material sense. Craig and Moreland overcome this potential pitfall by noting that this proposal assumes a part-whole relationship among the persons of the Trinity, without dividing the persons into individual instances of deity. Each person shares equally in the divine nature and must do so because tri-unity is intrinsic to the divine essence.[115] The implication of this description of the Godhead is that Nicene Christians direct their worship to the divine essence or nature, which is by definition tri-personal. As result, Nicene Christians worship deity as deity, which includes the divine persons of the Godhead.

In the final analysis, the only manner in which tritheists worship "one God" is by addressing their worship toward a unified set of individual, divine wills. Nicene Christians direct their adoration and worship to the divine nature, which is inherently Triune and tri-personal. In summation, Joseph Smith's tritheism results in the worship of either one being over another due to their level of divine attributes, or the adoration of a non-personal, immaterial collection of wills.

The Great Apostasy Considered

Joseph Smith's charge that a correct understanding of the Godhead had been lost by the early Christian church, and had consequently been absent for nearly 1800 years, is contingent upon a great falling away from truth among the first Christians. As previously stated, the biblical basis for this claim is considered to be rooted in the prophecy given in Amos 8:11–12. Yet, as will be seen, the aforementioned LDS interpretation does not withstand a careful approach to the text.

The context of this prophecy provides helpful information for understanding the intent of the author in penning this prophecy. Thomas McComiskey has written a rather compelling argument stating that the occasion of this prophecy surrounded the northern kingdom of Israel around 760 B.C. According to McComiskey it was the Assyrians who fulfilled this

115. Ibid.

prophecy later on, but since they are not mentioned in this text, it must be dated to a time earlier than their invasion. Further, Amos does not recognize or mention the rise of Tiglath-Pileser III who had a severe impact on Israel and Judah. These omissions fit within the framework of McComiskey's argument.[116] Furthermore, Amos only references Uzziah as reigning over Judah.[117] This is significant because around 750 B.C., Uzziah's son Jotham ascended to the position of co-regent. Thus, a 760 B.C. date for the time of this prophecy fits the known chronology of the period.[118]

Throughout the narrative, Amos announces the impending judgment of God upon both halves of the divided kingdom, Israel and Judah (Amos 1:3–2:16).[119] In the context of Amos 8:2–12, the same theme continues. According to Amos, the judgment to fall upon the people was for their failure to repent and turn from their sins. As James Luther Mays commented, the claim of Amos (8:11–12), following the judgment of God, is that the people of Israel would search for a word of promise and comfort from Yahweh but will find none. In context, the prophecy from Amos asserts that those desiring to hear from God will look from the "north to the east" (Amos 8:12). The intent of this message is that, although Judah would rise from judgment, and Yahweh would act upon Jerusalem, its central city of worship, the northern kingdom has no such hope.[120]

Similarly, Thomas Finley sees this entire process of seeking comfort from Yahweh as occurring from 745–722 B.C.[121] Finley's interpretation differs slightly from that of Mays, but both take into account the geographical cues found in the text. Both note that the language of the prophet, claiming that wandering occurs from the "north to the east," presents this search as taking place in a genuine geographical region during a specific time period. Likewise, Jorg Jeremias notes that the exiles from Israel should have travelled from the north to the east.[122] Additionally, F.F. Bruce writes that the

---

116. McComiskey, *The Expositor's Bible Commentary: Volume 7*, 275; Wood, *The Prophets of Israel*, 283–284; Bullock, *An Introduction to the Old Testament Prophetic Book*, 59–82.

117. Feinberg, *The Minor Prophets*, 86.

118. Archer, *A Survey of Old Testament Introduction*, 353.

119. Heschel. *The Prophets*, 30–31.

120. Mays, *Amos*, 149.

121. Finley, *Joel, Amos, Obadiah: An Exegetical Commentary*, 268.

122. Jeremias, *The Book of Amos*, 151.

steady encroachment of Assyria into the northern kingdom of Israel came from both the north and the east.[123]

Finley believed that while the judgment may have long-term ramifications, the focus of the prophecy is specifically fulfilled during the period of 745–722 B.C.[124] This interpretation is consistent with known language used to denote the latitudinal boundaries of the northern and southern kingdoms.[125] The implication of this interpretation is that the prophet assumes that the southern kingdom, Judah, will continue to have access to the words and blessings of Yahweh.[126] These data are confirmed by the fact that Amos also mentions Samaria, Dan, and Beersheba as the focus of this judgment. These locations had become centers of pagan activities among the kings in the north,[127] and are generally associated with the idolatry of the northern kingdom, such as the golden calves.[128]

The ramifications of this understanding of the prophecy delivered by Amos, which takes into account geographical and historical factors, are enormous. First, if the LDS interpretation is correct, then the Great Apostasy should have begun with the Assyrian captivity. However, this option for interpreting the prophecy is rather problematic because it would render the works of prophecy following the lifetime of Amos as having occurred during the era of apostasy. Moreover, the period of the incarnation and the apostolic age must also be tainted by the Great Apostasy. This most assuredly means that the entire New Testament and the latter portions of the Old Testament are corrupt.

Second, if the interpretation provided in this research is correct, then the LDS proposition of a Great Apostasy lacks the strength of its primary proof-text. Although this fact does not diminish the ability of prophetic LDS figures such as Joseph Smith to claim that there was, in fact, a period of apostasy following the apostolic age, this claim has to be supported by supposed continuing revelation, not enscripturated revelation. Consequently, the LDS insistence upon disregarding Nicene orthodoxy clarified in the early church lacks a basis in Christian Scripture.

123. Bruce, *Israel & the Nations*, 44.

124. Finley, *Joel, Amos, Obadiah: An Exegetical Commentary*, 268.

125. Walton et al., *The IVP Background Commentary of the Old Testament*, 772–773.

126. Paul and Cross, *Amos*, 266.

127. Matthews, *Old Testament Turning Points*, 113.

128. Walton et al., *The IVP Background Commentary of the Old Testament*, 773–774.

The interpretation of Amos provided in contrast to the LDS understanding is most plausible when considered in conjunction with the argumentation supplied in chapter 4. Despite claims to the contrary, Trinitarian theology has been present, at least in nascent form, since the apostolic age. Apostolic Fathers such as Clement speak of the existence of only one divine being (1 Clem, 46:6) who is revealed as Father, Son, and Spirit (1 Clem., 58). By the end of the apostolic age and with the dawn of apologetics writers, there was a concerted effort by Christian thinkers to defend the faith by asserting the oneness of God in being but plurality in persons (Haer., 2.1.2).

The advent of explicitly creedal, Trinitarian language is to be found in the writings of Tertullian (Apol., 21). The first to use the Nicene term Trinity, Tertullian (Praxaes, 2) stresses the uniqueness of each person of the Godhead while denying their substantive distinctions in terms of being. Furthermore, by the time of the Council of Nicaea in A.D. 325, the Trinitarian understanding of the Father, Son, and Spirit being co-equal was considered standard orthodoxy. The issue at Nicaea was not the establishment of a new orthodoxy over an older theological tradition; instead, Nicaea served to solidify the authority of historic orthodoxy over and above the new teachings of Arius. The content of "Nicene" orthodoxy did not find its genesis at Nicaea; instead, at Nicaea orthodoxy was clarified. The consistent teaching of the Christian church has been Nicene in nature from its inception. The evolution in doctrine has resulted not from innovation, but clarification as creedal precision has occurred.

The Problem of Eternal Regression

One of the primary faults of LDS tritheism rests in a philosophical absurdity to which its system inevitably leads. This absurdity is the inescapable conclusion of infinite god-regression. To state it simply, because God the Father is not the necessary, uncaused, cause of all things but is rather a finite creature who became exalted into a position of deity, there must be other gods who have experienced the same processes prior to Elohim. The LDS framework requires the existence of some type of eternal, material universe in which all other material universes exist. As will be demonstrated, this scenario results in LDS theology suffering from the impossibility of an actual infinite.

An actual infinite cannot exist in a tangible, genuine sense. A good analogy of this fact is seen within the illustration known as Hilbert's Hotel.

The premise of Hilbert's Hotel is that there exists a hotel that contains an infinite number of rooms for an infinite number of guests. This well-known illustration is historically argued as follows: Upon arriving at Hilbert's Hotel, guests find an infinite number of rooms; thus, a new guest seeking a room is informed that all of these rooms are in fact full because the infinite number of rooms are currently occupied by an infinite number of guests.[129] But the clerk is most accommodating and asks that all guests shift over by one room, thereby freeing one room for this new guest.[130] Because there are an infinite number of rooms, it becomes possible to shift every person filling these rooms and there will still be more rooms.[131]

As William Lane Craig points out, the strange thing about this illustration is that such a process of accommodation could be repeated for an infinite number of guests and yet the hotel would never gain any more guests (in terms of total numbers) than were present upon the arrival of the first guest mentioned above.[132] Stranger still is the fact that even if guests leave the hotel, all of the rooms remain full because of the infinite number of guests occupying the infinite number of rooms.[133] In short, Hilbert's Hotel can in one instant have empty rooms yet be entirely full! It is an absurdity. This demonstrates that an infinite regression of aggregative finite structures cannot exist in a material universe.[134]

Just as the preceding illustration indicates the absurdity of an actual infinite, so does the reality of the present. The reader will readily agree upon the reality of their existence in the present. However, if an actual infinite regression of gods is true, and if the universe is also infinite, then the present could never have become a reality. The logic behind this proposition is simple: one could never span the successive and infinite series of events that preceded today. As J.P. Moreland noted, if an individual attempts to span an infinite number of days from the past to reach the present, that individual cannot help but fail. Why? Because in an infinite regression of days, one could never move in reverse to the beginning of days or from the

---

129. Craig, "The Kalām Cosmological Argument," 26.

130. Ibid; Oppy, *Philosophical Perspectives on Infinity*, 8–9.

131. Clark, *Paradoxes from A to Z*, 94; Higgins, *Numbers: A Very Short Introduction*, 85–86.

132. Craig, "The Kalām Cosmological Argument," 27–28.

133. Craig and Copan, *Creation Our of Nothing*, 201–203.

134. Spitzer, *New Proofs for the Existence of God*, 200.

beginning to the present, because there exists an infinite number of days between the two points.[135]

Applying this logic to the problem at hand reveals the following: If there were an infinite number of gods, each one material and bound by time, who preceded Elohim in the progression to godhood, Elohim could never become a god, and today would never become a reality. The cause of this problem is rather straightforward: an infinite progression requires an infinite number of gods and an infinite number of days between the infinite past and the present.[136] Since the gulf of time and gods could never be traversed because there would always be one more god that must come before Elohim or one more day before arriving at the present, then, in fact Elohim could never become a god, and today could never be actualized. In short, Elohim would be stuck in the absurdity of an infinite regression with no hope of reaching the present. However, because the present is an actual reality, there cannot be an infinite regression of gods and days preceding the present.

CONCLUSION

The aim of this chapter has been to adequately address the following research question: What was Smith's doctrine of God and how has this doctrine been revised or clarified by LDS leadership over nearly two centuries into its modern formulation? The answer to this question has been arrived at through the following avenues. First, it was demonstrated that the sources of LDS doctrine are somewhat fluid, but have their primary authority rooted in Mormon Scripture and the pronouncements of Joseph Smith. Second, it was explained that the teachings of the LDS leadership, including prophets, apostles, and scholars, have had some influence in clarifying and expanding on the tritheism proposed by Joseph Smith. The elements of theology discussed were those that reflected the central teachings of Joseph Smith. So, while the LDS leaders and thinkers cited often expanded upon the words of Joseph Smith, they were grounded in their basic commitment to the core elements of Smith's tritheism.

Third, it was established that early LDS publications and Scripture seem to teach a modalistic understanding of the Godhead. Yet, this initially monotheistic and sometimes Trinitarian verbiage is not a problem

135. Moreland, *Scaling the Secular City*, 29.

136. Ibid; Geisler and Corduan, *Philosophy of Religion*, 184.

for Mormonism. Because the Mormon system includes a commitment to ever-progressing revelation, the problem of the initially orthodox language in early Mormonism and the Book of Mormon can be readily dismissed. Fourth, contemporary LDS scholarship was engaged to provide current data regarding Mormon doctrinal discussions in the realm of academia.

A further foray was taken into the LDS belief in a Great Apostasy. This LDS position proposes that the need for Joseph Smith's tritheism arises out of the falling away of Christendom from genuine apostolic doctrine. According to LDS sources, the initial doctrine of God taught by the Apostles mirrors Smith's doctrine instead of that found in the Nicene tradition.

The information gleaned from answering the research questions guiding this chapter led to a threefold assessment of Smith's theology. First, it was demonstrated that Joseph Smith's theology underwent a period of development resulting in tritheism. This tritheism found its most explicit scriptural backing in Joseph Smith's supposed translation of the *Book of Abraham*. However, the 1967 recovery of the papyri, which were the basis for the *Book of Abraham*, revealed that what Smith allegedly translated was a combination of fragments from the Egyptian Book of Breathings and the Book of the Dead.

Second, the basis for the supposed Great Apostasy was engaged at a textual level. It was indicated that the supposed prophecy of the corruption of Christendom was actually a prophecy regarding the fall of the northern kingdom of Israel. Based upon the references to pagan deities and geographical cues, the only consistent interpretation of the passage is that Amos had the fall of the northern kingdom to Assyria in view. Additionally, the reader was reminded of the consistently Trinitarian theology of the early church as discussed in chapter 3. While not always finely tuned with creedal language, from the apostolic age forward Christianity has always been Nicene in theology, if not in name.

Third, the corollary of Smith's tritheism is the eternal progression of human beings into positions of deity. These deities take for themselves worlds of their own to rule as gods. This proposition leads to an eternal regression of gods. It was demonstrated that although infinite regression can be proposed or theorized, an actual infinite regression cannot exist. In short, if there is an infinite regression of gods prior to the exaltation and deification of Elohim, then the universe in which Elohim is God would never be actualized. Why? Because if an infinite regression of gods is true, there must always be one more god needing to progress prior to the deification of Elohim.

In conclusion, the primary means of progress and the basis for Smith's tritheism is founded upon less than historically, scripturally, or philosophically strong ground. It has been demonstrated that Smith's theology is rather fluid in nature and unsound in argumentation. What remains to be accomplished is a necessary conclusion to the present research. In keeping with scholarly research procedures, the conclusion to come will provide a conservative estimate of what this project has succeeded in accomplishing and will note areas necessitating further research.

Chapter 6

Conclusion

INTRODUCTION

The central argument of this research project has been that Joseph Smith was one of a number of people in his region and of his era who abandoned historic, Nicene Christianity. Therefore, modern LDS formulations, as well as Smith's tritheism, should be evaluated and criticized in the light of historic, Nicene orthodoxy founded on proper exegesis of Scripture. We have achieved this aim by means of utilizing church history, American history, exegesis, and philosophy in examining and criticizing the development of Joseph Smith's tritheism. The purpose of the present chapter is to synthesize the conclusions of the previous chapters in order to tie together the outcome of this study.

JOSEPH SMITH'S TRITHEISM IN LIGHT OF NICENE ORTHODOXY GROUNDED IN THE CHRISTIAN SCRIPTURES

Much of what was uncovered in chapter 3 arises from answering the following questions. First, what is the basis of Nicene orthodoxy? Second, what is the clear, systematic teaching of Scripture regarding the doctrine of the Trinity?

The data examined demonstrate that the consistent biblical teaching delivered among the early Israelites was staunchly monotheistic. This insistence upon monotheism stands in distinction to the polytheistic milieu in which Hebrew religion took its shape.[1] Thus, much of the theological content of the Pentateuch is focused on the affirmation of monotheism.[2] Nevertheless, Nicene Christians have historically interpreted certain Old Testament references as direct allusions to the triune nature of the Godhead. Instances of note include both plural and triadic references to deity found throughout the Old Testament (Gen. 1:26; 11:7; Num. 6:24–26; Isa. 6:3; 33:2; Hag. 2:5–7; Dan. 7:9). Historically, the Nicene position maintains that the Old Testament references to God only make consistent sense if understood in light of the explicit, New Testament doctrine of the Trinity.

In the Nicene tradition, the Old Testament reveals the doctrine of the Trinity implicitly while the New Testament teaches the doctrine explicitly, largely via narrative. Perhaps the clearest demonstration of the shift from Old Testament theism to Trinitarianism, asserted via narrative, is seen in the distinction between the Father and the Son.[3] With the incarnation of Jesus as God the Son, there is an identifiable plurality of persons who are the one God of the Old Testament (Deut. 6:4). In fact, the Father-Son relationship of persons in the Godhead is referenced in all but three letters of the New Testament.[4] In the Gospel narratives alone, this relationship between Father and Son is noted 275 times. The prime example of this Father-Son relationship is seen in the unique way in which Jesus addressed the Father in prayer.[5]

Beyond the familial relationship of the Father and Son presented in the New Testament, the portrayal of the Son as God is quite compelling. In the prologue of John, the Word (Jesus) is referred to as *theos* or God (John 1:1). In fact, John 1:1–3 refers to the Word as *theos*, but then also states that the Word was with God (*pros ton theon*). The implication is that while there is only one God, He is multi-personal. Throughout the synoptics and John's narratives, the deity of Jesus is either taught or implied. For instance, the account of Jesus walking on water (Matt. 14:25; Mark 6:48; John 6:19) is found in three the Gospels. This particular account implicitly points to the deity of Christ because the Old Testament clearly states that Yahweh alone

---

1. Rofe, *Old Testament Studies: Deuteronomy*, 19; Miles, *A God of Many Understandings?*, 59–62.

2. Sailhamer, *The Pentateuch as Narrative*, 285; Frame, *The Doctrine of God*, 622–623.

3. Cooper, *Our Father in Heaven*, 108.

4. Coppedge, *Our Triune God*, 27.

5. Jeremias, *The Prayers of Jesus*, 57.

has power over the sea (Psalm 107:23–32; Isa. 43:16), and Yahweh alone can walk on the waters (Job 9:8). Elsewhere in the New Testament, Jesus is spoken of as *eikōn tou theou tou aoratou* (Col. 1:15). He is literally the mirror image of God the Father. Yet, the New Testament authors are careful to note that the Father-Son relationship and the shared nature of deity does not imply a time-space, biological origination of the Son. Rather, the relationship of the Son to the Father speaks of the one-of-a-kind relationship that Jesus has with God the Father. This is why the Son's relationship to the Father is described as *monogenēs* and not *monogennetos*.[6]

The biblical authors go beyond assigning deity to just the Father and the Son by also referring to the Holy Spirit as God. Matthew's Gospel connects the role of the Spirit as equal in the baptismal formulation occurring in Matt. 28:19. Mark records Jesus preaching against blaspheming the Holy Spirit, which must make him God because Scripture categorizes blasphemy as something that can only be committed against God. Additionally, the Spirit is described as exercising attributes that only deity can possess (1 Cor. 2:10–11; Psalm 139). Thus, with the background of Old Testament monotheism, there is a new dynamic in the completion of the text of the New Testament: a multi-personal God.

JOSEPH SMITH'S TRITHEISM IN LIGHT OF NICENE ORTHODOXY GROUNDED IN THE CHRISTIAN SCRIPTURES: CONCLUSION

Because it is foundational, the importance of these data in assessing the tritheism of Joseph Smith cannot be overstated. Let us remind ourselves of the information we acquired in the course of chapter 3. What can be ascertained from the textual data is that the authors of the Christian Scripture argued for the existence of one deity, God. However, they further attributed tri-personality to this being in the persons of Father, Son, and Holy Spirit. Without question, there is a tension present in the affirmation of one God (qualitatively) and three persons (relationally). Yet, this is precisely what the content of Scripture naturally leads the reader to understand as being descriptive of the divine being. Therefore, the content of the Christian Scripture provides the necessary revelatory support for Nicene orthodoxy.

---

6. Carson, *Exegetical Fallacies*, 30; White, *The King James Only Controversy*, 201–202; Thielman, *Theology of the New Testament*, 154.

JOSEPH SMITH'S TRITHEISM IN LIGHT OF THE
HISTORICAL DEVELOPMENT OF NICENE ORTHODOXY

The interaction with the Christian Scripture as the basis for Nicene orthodoxy demonstrates the theological ground in which creedal, Nicene orthodoxy grew. As argued in chapter 3, the creedal formulations of Nicene orthodoxy took shape over an extended period of time. However, the earliest Christians held to the central elements of Nicene orthodoxy as revealed in the Christian Scripture. Thus, historical inquiry confirms that there has never been a time in which Nicene orthodoxy (at least in nascent form) was not synonymous with apostolic doctrine.[7]

Prior to A.D. 100, both Clement (I Clem. 46:6; 58) and Ignatius (Mag., 13) wrote to Christians, speaking of there being only one God while referring to Him using a triadic schema. By the middle of the second century, Justin Martyr was actively defending Christianity by arguing for the persons of the Godhead as sharing in the divine nature (I Apol., 63), while remaining one being and distinct in personhood (Dial., 61). In the same period, Athenagoras defended Christianity against paganism by arguing that orthodox Christians are monotheists (Plea., 10). By the close of the second century, Irenaeus argued that the triunity of the one God is a necessarily belief, because the plan of redemption is grounded in the tripersonality of God.[8]

Moving beyond the second century and into the third, it is noteworthy that even theologians such as Origen, in his commentary on John (2.6), spoke of God as a plurality of hypostases, but only one in being. During this same period, Tertullian would coin the term Trinity and enter it into the orthodox theological lexicon. Similar to Origen, Tertullian (Apol., 21) argued that there is one being (God) but there are three persons who share equally and totally in the nature of that one being. Thus, even prior to the council of Nicaea in A.D. 325 Christians already adhered to a rather developed form of Trinitarianism.

Following the Council of Nicaea's affirmation and restatement of historic, apostolic Christian doctrine, orthodox theologians reached new levels in creedal explanations of the Trinity. Significantly, Gregory of Nyssa penned a work, *On Not Three Gods*, specifically aimed at curtailing the

---

7. Rusch, *The Trinitarian Controversy*, 3.

8. Lohse, *A Short History of Christian Doctrine*, 44; Torrance, *The Christian Doctrine of God*, 75.

accusation that Christians were tritheists. Gregory asserted that the persons of the Godhead are not merely unified in purpose but derive their nature as deity by being one in essence (Tres dii). While Gregory acknowledges that some misunderstand the biblical teaching of three persons to imply three gods, Gregory argued that such an interpretation fails to synthesize the full content of Scripture coherently.[9] Augustine further described the orthodox understanding of the Trinity by stating that no single person of the Godhead could be called "God."[10] Rather, triunity is intrinsic to deity in such a way that only a single being that is plural in persons could ever be rightly referred to as God (Trin., 5.9). Therefore, the doctrine of the Trinity revealed in Scripture is not a mere collection of deified individuals acting as one God, but one God revealed in three distinct persons.

JOSEPH SMITH'S TRITHEISM IN LIGHT OF THE HISTORICAL DEVELOPMENT OF NICENE ORTHODOXY: CONCLUSION

The weight of history stands against the claim by Joseph Smith that early Christians were actually tritheists. The conclusion, based on the facts reported in chapters 2 and 3, is simply this: Christian orthodoxy has always been "Nicene." Trinitarianism, at least in nascent form, has been the orthodox approach to understanding the Godhead since the advent of the church. Because Christianity has been Nicene in its theology proper from the apostolic era, any attempt to understand or explain the Godhead that does not adhere to the bounds of orthodoxy established in the Old and New Testaments, and affirmed through creeds in the early church, ought to be understood as an unorthodox and distinct break from historic Christianity.

JOSEPH SMITH'S TRITHEISM IN LIGHT OF HIS HISTORICAL CONTEXT

Taking into consideration the conclusions presented thus far, what specific factors could be pointed to in establishing how and why Joseph Smith broke from historic, Nicene orthodoxy? The bulk of this information was

9. Ayers, *Nicaea and its Legacy*, 360.
10. Hill, *The History of Christian Thought*, 87.

examined in chapter 5. However, it is pertinent to present a synthesis of these data and their conclusion.

Joseph Smith's tritheism must be recognized as developing somewhat naturally out of his historical context. With the dawn of the eighteenth century in North America came a renewed desire for liberty. Colonists had begun resenting the unfair taxation they were enduring under the rule of Great Britain, and for some the total independence from the Old World was necessary. In the midst of this scenario, the theological rule of the day was largely orthodox, due in part to the influence of the Puritans. However, there arose an anti-orthodox sentiment resulting from the mingling of ecclesiastical and governmental powers in the Old World.

A pivotal change in North American religion occurred in early eighteenth century with the outbreak of the Great Awakening. While initially precipitated under the preaching of Jonathan Edwards,[11] it was to be the itinerant preaching of George Whitefield[12] that would carry the excitement and religious enthusiasm of the Great Awakening across North America. A number of the results of the Great Awakening were positive and included a renewed interest in the gospel. However, some of the transformative results were a disregard for traditional orthodoxy and an emphasis upon moving from a clergy-centered to a laity-centered ecclesiology.[13]

The most significant consequence was the development of Christian Republicanism, the idea that ordained clergy did not occupy a privileged position in determining what was true and proper in religion.[14] It was Christian Republicanism that galvanized religious institutions in their support of independence. However, the blending of religiosity with the ideals of republicanism led to a negative outlook upon the perceived tyranny of traditional, Nicene institutions. For the purpose of this research, one of the most significant findings is that many of the religious movements fuelling Christian Republicanism were either heterodox at best, or anti-Trinitarian at worst.[15]

In the years following the American Revolution, there arose an increasing number of alternative and unorthodox religious movements.[16] The

11. Noll, *The Rise of Evangelicalism*, 77–78.

12. Ahlstrom, *A Religious History of the American People*, 283.

13. Noll, *America's God*, 48–49; Sweet, *The Story of Religion in America*, 134.

14. Sandoz, *Republicanism, Religion, and the Soul of America*, 6.

15. Clark, *The Language of Liberty 1660–1832*, 38–39.

16. Ahlstrom, *A Religious History of the American People*, 356–357.

influence of these movements, Christian Republicanism, and new religious attitudes had a lasting impact upon Joseph Smith's family. Smith's grandparents, his uncle Jason, and his parents all adhered to, dabbled in, or were committed to unorthodox and even anti-Trinitarian movements.

Furthermore, in the same areas that Joseph Smith and his family frequented there were numerous anti-Nicene sects.[17] Briefly, these groups included Isaac Bullard's "Pilgrims," who organized their movement within a few minutes' walk from the Smith residence in Vermont. Bullard, who claimed to be a prophet, encouraged "free love," preached the imminent end of all things, and eventually led his followers on the same migration path that the Latter Day Saints would later travel under Smith's direction.[18]

Another probable influence upon Smith's theological formation is that of Jemima Wilkinson. While possibly claiming to have been Jesus in female form, Wilkinson clearly believed herself to be a prophetess who disregarded traditional marriage and was bent on restoring true doctrine to the earth. Even more striking is that Wilkinson's community existed just twenty-five miles from Smith's Palmyra home and was often referred to in the Palmyra newspaper.[19]

Beyond the probable influences of Bullard or Wilkinson, Joseph Smith was admittedly familiar with the Shakers.[20] Holding to an unorthodox view of sexuality, the Shakers established their community in New York, not far from Palmyra.[21] As a group that rejected much of traditional, historic orthodoxy, the Shakers undoubtedly influenced the young Joseph Smith.

Perhaps even more compelling than the known probable influences of alternative movements upon Joseph Smith were the popular visionaries of the day with whom he had contact. Many of these supposed visionaries would either pass through Palmyra and adjacent towns or have their visions published and thus made accessible to people in Palmyra, New York. The central elements of many of these visions are found in Smith's own First Vision. Included in these details are reports of seeing the Father and Jesus while praying in the woods and being informed that all the churches of the Christendom are corrupt.[22]

---

17. Newman, *The Real History of the End of the World*, 184.

18. Ibid, 210–211.

19. Wisbey, *Pioneer Prophetess*, 21; Brodie, *No Man Knows My History*, 13.

20. *D&C* 49:1

21. Gutek and Gutek, *Visiting Utopian Communities*, 33.

22. Bushman, *Joseph Smith: Rough Stone Rolling*, 60; Abanes, *One Nation Under*

JOSEPH SMITH'S TRITHEISM IN LIGHT OF HIS HISTORICAL CONTEXT: CONCLUSION

It is inconceivable that Smith's thought was not to a great extent shaped by the beliefs of his own family. Varying degrees of unorthodox theology and anti-Nicene sentiments permeated the Smith bloodline. Moreover, throughout Joseph's formative years, he was in consistently close proximity with anti-Nicene movements and teachers. Additionally, Smith's First Vision account borrows heavily from details of supposed visions that were widely reported in his area. Therefore, Smith's tritheism must be understood as a consequence of his family's influence as well as his historical, religious context.

JOSEPH SMITH'S TRITHEISM IN LDS LITERATURE

The scriptural support for Smith's tritheism is rooted in the Book of Mormon and *The Pearl of Great Price*. Yet, as discussed in chapter 5, the content of the Book of Mormon reflects a somewhat orthodox or Nicene understanding of the Godhead. In the Book of Mormon, much of the material on the nature of God alternates between Trinitarian language and modalism.[23] Given that Smith's theology evolved over a period of time, this confusion fits with the previously mentioned conclusions derived from the data examined in previous chapters.

Near the time of the publication of the Book of Mormon, Smith was still espousing a somewhat orthodox understanding of the Godhead.[24] In fact, Smith's attempt to re-translate the book of Genesis in 1830, was heavily monotheistic when referring to the Godhead. It was not until the period between 1832 and 1833 that Smith began explicitly denying orthodoxy as it related to the nature of God. By 1838, Smith was routinely proclaiming a tritheistic understanding of the Godhead by asserting his belief in a plurality of gods.[25] To validate this decisive move from orthodoxy, Smith posited a great falling away from apostolic doctrine in the early church. According to Smith, Amos 8:11–12 represents a prophecy regarding a Great Apostasy, which was fulfilled shortly after the death of the Apostle John. Further bol-

---

Gods, 21.

23. Vogel, "The Earliest Mormon Concept of God," 17–33.

24. *D&C* 20:17–28

25. *D&C* 121:32

stering his claims against orthodoxy, Smith produced a new text supporting his theology. In 1842, Smith began "translating" ancient papyri that he claimed were written by Abraham. In the course of his translation, Smith referred to the Godhead as "gods" forty-eight times. Then in 1844 an article appeared in the LDS publication *Times and Seasons*, where Smith expressly taught tritheism as the orthodox Mormon position.[26]

The translation of the Book of Abraham represented the textual support Smith needed in order to prescribe the worship of three gods who acted as one God while existing among a plurality of divine beings as dogma. However, as was explored in chapter 5, the content of the papyri translated by Smith as the Book of Abraham were actually Egyptian funerary texts.[27] Therefore, Smith's much-needed scriptural support for his tritheism has been demonstrated not to be a translation at all, but an utter forgery.

JOSEPH SMITH'S TRITHEISM IN LDS LITERATURE: CONCLUSION

Provided that Smith's theology underwent a clear and historically identifiable development, the material uncovered in chapter 5 confirms the conclusion derived from the previous chapters. Smith's tritheism was a result of his own fertile imagination under the life-long influences from outside the bounds of Nicene orthodoxy. Smith's claims regarding the prophecy of Amos 8:11–12 have been demonstrated to be untrue. The fact that this prophecy is verifiably fulfilled in the Assyrian captivity undermines Smith's entire premise for "restoring" supposedly apostolic doctrine. Additionally, the clear Nicene content of Christian doctrine from the time of the Apostles and beyond (chapter 3) is consistent with the conclusions of this research, but not with the claims of Joseph Smith. Furthermore, Smith's theology is philosophically incoherent. As discussed in chapter 5, the necessary implication of Smith's theology is that of an eternal regression of gods. However, the existence of an actual infinite is both impossible and demonstrated to be false by the existence of the present. Therefore, the conclusion of this section of data is that Smith's move from orthodoxy to heterodoxy and then eventually to tritheism was fuelled by his own desire to create a religion to rival Nicene orthodoxy.

26. Roberts, *History of the Church: Volume 6*, 474.

27. Baer, "The Breathing Permit of Hor," 111–118; Rhodes, "A Translation and Commentary of the Joseph Smith Hypocephalus," 265.

FINAL CONCLUSIONS

This research project has achieved its aim in establishing that Nicene orthodoxy is grounded in the consistent teaching of the Christian Scripture on the nature of God. Decisively monotheistic in content, the Scriptures also reveal a plurality of divine persons. Nicene orthodoxy has historically sought to express this truth through creedal affirmations of the biblical content. The resulting Nicene theology has stood as the core of orthodoxy for nearly 2,000 years. Leading up to and following the American Revolution, there was a development of anti-Nicene attitudes and alternative religious movements. Joseph Smith was born into a period when people were preoccupied with religious excitement and unorthodox theology. Much of what Smith would later espouse can be directly and historically traced to a variety of theological contacts and influences during this period. He eventually attempted to undergird his theological proclamations with philosophically incoherent prophetic utterances and forgeries passed off as translations. Therefore, the result of prudent research reveals that Joseph Smith is neither a unique prophet nor a skilled theologian. Instead, the final analysis demonstrates Joseph Smith to be merely one of many would-be unorthodox religious founders of his era. Yet, the success of his unorthodox community and its impact upon religion in North America cannot be denied.

FURTHER RESEARCH

A number of disciplines and investigative approaches have been employed throughout the course of this project. However, no single research effort can entail all of the necessary avenues of study for thoroughly engaging any such topic. Therefore, areas necessitating further inquiry beyond the contents of the present project ought to be briefly mentioned.

Further Research: The Origins of the Book of Mormon

Important details of Joseph Smith's evolving theology have been scrutinized. Further, the rather orthodox theology in the Book of Mormon has been noted. Still, much more can and should be done in terms of researching the theological content of the Book of Mormon as it relates to the theological convictions of Joseph Smith during the period of its compilation.

Two volumes of note are David Persuitte's *Joseph Smith and the Origins of the Book of Mormon* (2000) and Cowdery, Davis, and Vanick's *Who Really Wrote the Book of Mormon?* (2005). While both of these volumes go to great lengths to discover the literature from which Smith possibly derived the content of the Book of Mormon, neither text attempts to trace the theological themes of the Book of Mormon in connection to Smith's own theological development within researchable, historical data. In order to address Smith's theological evolution adequately, this area of research has to be engaged.

Further Research: Smith's Philosophy of Religion

The present project explores the lack of philosophical coherence inherent to Smith's tritheism. In the past, Nicene thinker Francis Beckwith has undertaken a full-fledged attempt to evaluate LDS theology in regards to philosophical coherence.[28] Recently, Beckwith acted as one of three editors for a volume entitled, *The New Mormon Challenge* (2002). The latter title briefly interacts with the philosophical basis of a number of elements inherent to the LDS worldview. As helpful as Beckwith's efforts have been, there needs to be a thorough engagement of Smith's theology and worldview based upon its philosophical coherence. Such an endeavor should further provide insights into the potential influences upon Smith's own theology and worldview. Additionally, the results of this proposed area of investigation would be beneficial in further solidifying the stark contrasts between the theology and worldview of Nicene Christianity and that of Joseph Smith.

FINAL THOUGHTS

The findings of this project will serve as a reminder of the dramatically unorthodox claims of Joseph Smith and his attempt to develop a religious system intent on supplanting Nicene Christianity. However, as the suggestions for further research demonstrate, the range of potential research regarding Joseph Smith's theological development has not been exhausted. Nicene thinkers must continue to interact with Joseph Smith's theology, life, and worldview in order to provide meaningful appraisals of both Smith and the church he founded.

---

28. Beckwith and Parrish, *The Mormon Concept of God.*

Bibliography

Abanes, Richard. *One Nation Under Gods*. New York, NY: Four Walls Eight Windows, 2003.

———. *Becoming Gods*. Eugene, OR: Harvest House, 2004.

Athenagoras. "A Plea for the Christians," in Vol. 2 of *The Ante-Nicene Fathers*, edited by Alexander Roberts and James Donaldson, 123–148. Peabody, MA: Hendrickson Publishers, 2004.

Augustine. "Confessions," in Vol. 1 of *The Nicene and Post-Nicene Fathers: Second Series*, edited by Phillip Schaff, 45–208. Peabody, MA: Hendrickson Publishers, 2004.

———. "On the Faith and Creed," in Vol. 3 of *The Nicene and Post-Nicene Fathers: First Series*, edited by Phillip Schaff, 321–333. Peabody, MA: Hendrickson Publishers, 2004.

———. "On the Holy Trinity," in Vol. 3 of *The Nicene and Post-Nicene Fathers: First Series*, edited by Phillip Schaff, 1–228. Peabody, MA: Hendrickson Publishers, 2004.

Ahlstrom, Sydney. *A Religious History of the American People*. London: Yale University Press, 1972.

Allan, Gordon. "Southcottian Sects from 1790 to the Present Day." In *Expecting the End: Millennialism in Social and Historical Context*, edited by Kenneth Newport and Crawford Gribben, 213–215. Waco, TX: Baylor University Press, 2006.

Allis, Oswald. *God Spake by Moses*. Phillipsburg, NJ: P&R Publishing, 1951.

Allison, Greg. *Historical Theology*. Grand Rapids, MI: Zondervan Academic, 2011.

Anderson, Bernhard, and Steve Bishop. *Contours of Old Testament Theology*. Minneapolis, MN: Augsburg Fortress Press, 1999.

Anderson, Ross. *Understanding the Book of Mormon*. Grand Rapids, MI: Zondervan, 2009.

Anderson, Richard. *Understanding Paul*. Salt Lake City, UT: Deseret Books, 2010.

Aquinas, Thomas. *Summa Theologica: Volume 1, Part 1*. New York, NY: Cosimo Classics, 2013.

Archer, Gleason. *A Survey of Old Testament Introduction*. Chicago, IL: Moody Press, 1994.

Ayers, Lewis. *Nicaea and its Legacy: An Approach to Fourth-Century Trinitarian Theology*. New York, NY: Oxford University Press, 2006.

———. *Augustine and the Trinity*. New York, NY: Cambridge University Press, 2010.

Barnard, Leslie. *Théologie Historique: Athenagoras*. Paris, France: Éditions Beauchesne, 1972.

Baer, Klaus. "The Breathing Permit of Hor." *Dialogue: A Journal of Mormon Thought* 3(1968):111–127.

Bibliography

Bauckham, Richard. *God Crucified: Monotheism and Christology in the New Testament.* Carlisle: Paternoster, 1998.

Bavinck, Herman. *Reformed Dogmatics: Abridged.* Grand Rapids, MI: Baker Academic, 2011.

Beale, G.K., and D.A. Carson, eds. *Commentary on the New Testament Use of the Old Testament.* Grand Rapids, MI: Baker Academic, 2007.

Bebbington, David. *Evangelicalism in Modern Britain.* London: Routledge, 1989.

———. *The Dominance of Evangelicalism.* Downers Grove, IL: InterVarsity Press, 2005.

Becking, Bob., ed. *Only One God?: Monotheism in Ancient Israel and the Veneration of the Goddess Asherah.* London: Sheffield Academic Press, 2001.

Beckwith, Francis, and Stephen Parrish. *See the Gods Fall.* College Press Publishing Company, 2000.

———, Carl Mosser, and Paul Owen, eds. *The New Mormon Challenge.* Grand Rapids, MI: Zondervan, 2002.

Beneke, Chris. *Beyond Toleration.* New York: Oxford University Press, 2006.

Berkhof, Louis. *The History of Christian Doctrines.* Carlisle, PA: Banner of Truth Trust, 1996.

Bergera, Gary, ed. *Line Upon Line: Essays on Mormon Doctrine.* Salt Lake City, UT: Signature Books, 1989.

Berliner, A, and Israel Drazin, trans. *Targum Onqelos to Exodus.* KTAV Publishing House, 1990.

Blomberg, Craig. *Jesus and the Gospels.* Nashville, TN: B&H, 1997.

———, and Stephen Robinson. *How Wide the Divide?* Downers Grove, IL: InterVarsity Press, 1997.

———. *The Historical Reliability of John's Gospel: Issues & Commentary.* Downers Grove, IL: InterVarsity Press, 2001.

Bock, Darrell. *Jesus According to Scripture.* Grand Rapids, MI: Baker Academic, 2002.

Bowman, Robert, and Ed Komoszewski. *Putting Jesus in His Place.* Grand Rapids, MI: Kregel Publications, 2007.

Bray, Gerald. *The Doctrine of God.* Downers Grove, IL: InterVarsity Press, 1993.

———. *God is Love: A Biblical and Systematic Theology.* Wheaton, IL: Crossway, 2012.

Bright, John. *A History of Israel.* Louisville, KY: John Knox Press, 2000.

Brodie, Fawn. *No Man Knows My History: The Life of Joseph Smith.* New York, NY: Vintage Books, 1995.

Brown, Harold. *Heresies: Heresy and Orthodoxy in the History of the Church.* Peabody, MA: Hendrickson Publishers, 2003.

Bruce, F.F. *Israel & the Nations.* Downers Grove, IL: InterVarsity Press, 1997.

Bullock, Hassell. *An Introduction to the Old Testament Prophetic Books.* Chicago, IL: Moody Press, 1986.

Bushman, Richard. *Joseph Smith and the Beginnings of Mormonism.* Champaign, IL: University of Illinois Press, 1988.

———. *Joseph Smith: Rough Stone Rolling.* New York: Vintage Books, 2007.

Butler, Jon, Grant Wacker, and Randall Balmer. *Religion in American Life.* New York: Oxford University Press, 2011.

Cairns, Earle. *Christianity Through the Centuries: A History of the Christian Church.* Grand Rapids, MI: Zondervan, 1996.

Calvin, John. *Institutes of Christian Religion.* Translated by Henry Beveridge. Peabody, MA: Hendrickson Publishing, 2008.

Carson, D.A. "Matthew" in Vol. 8 of *The Expositor's Bible Commentary,* edited by Frank Gaebelein, 3–602. Grand Rapids, MI: Zondervan, 1984.

————. *Exegetical Fallacies.* Grand Rapids, MI: Baker Academic, 1996.

Caswall, Henry. *The Prophet of the Nineteenth Century.* London: J.G.F. & J. Rivington, 1843.

Chadwick, Henry. *The Early Church.* New York: Penguin Books, 1993.

Clark, J.C.D. *The Language of Liberty 1660–1832.* Cambridge University Press, 1994.

Clark, Michael. *Paradoxes from A to Z.* New York: Routledge, 2007.

Clement. "I Clement," in Vol. 9 of *The Ante-Nicene Fathers,* edited by Allan Menzies, 229–248. Peabody, MA: Hendrickson Publishers, 2004.

Clines, David. *On the Way to the Postmodern: Old Testament Essays, 1967–1998.* Sheffield, England: Sheffield Academic Press, 1998.

Corduan, Winfried. *A Tapestry of Faiths.* Downers Grove, IL: InterVarsity Press, 2002.

————. *In the Beginning God.* Nashville, TN: B&H Academic, 2013.

Cornett, Daryl, *ed. Christian America?* Nashville, TN: B&H Academic, 2011.

Cooper, John. *Our Father in Heaven.* Grand Rapids, MI: Baker, 1998.

Coppedge, Allan. *The God Who is Triune.* Downers Grove, IL: InterVarsity Press Academic, 2007.

Cowdery, Oliver. *Messenger and Advocate.* 3–5(1834):42–79.

Cowdery, Wayne, Howard Davis, and Arthur Vanick. *Who Really Wrote the Book of Mormon?* St. Louis, MO: Concordia Publishing House, 2005.

Craig, William Lane. "The Kalām Cosmological Argument." In *Philosophy of Religion,* edited by Louis Pojman, 24–30. Belmont, CA: Wadsworth Publishing House, 1998.

————, *ed.* 2002. *Philosophy of Religion.* New Brunswick, NJ: Rutgers University Press. 634 p.

————, and J.P. Moreland. *Philosophical Foundations for a Christian Worldview.* Downers Grove, IL: InterVarsity Press, 2003.

————, Paul Copan. *Creation Out of Nothing.* Grand Rapids, MI: Baker Academic, 2004.

Origen. *Treatise on the Passover ; And, Dialogue of Origen with Heraclides.* Edited by R.J. Daly. Mahwah, NJ: Paulist Press, 1992.

Davila, James, Carey Newman, and Gladys Lewis, ed. *The Jewish Roots of Christological Monotheism.* Leiden, The Netherlands: Brill, 1999.

Davis, Leo. *The First Seven Ecumenical Councils.* Collegeville, MN. Liturgical Press, 1990.

Dunn, Geoffrey. *Tertullian.* New York, NY: Routledge, 2007.

Dyrness, William. *Themes in Old Testament Theology.* Downers Grove, IL: InterVarsity Press, 1979.

Eedgar, William, and Scott Oliphint, *eds. Christian Apologetics: Past and Present.* Wheaton, IL: Crossway, 2009.

Edwards, Jonathon. *The Works of Jonathan Edwards: Volume 21.* Edited by Sang Hyun Lee. Grand Rapids, MI: Yale University Press, 2003.

Eichrodt, Walther. *Theology of the Old Testament: Volume I.* Louisville, KY: John Know Press, 1967.

Ellis, Edward. *The Old Testament in Early Christianity.* Grand Rapids, MI: Baker Book House, 1992.

Erhman, Bart. *Christianity in Late Antiquity.* New York: Oxford University Press, 2004.

————. *Misquoting Jesus.* New York: HarperCollins, 2007.

Fairbairn, Donald. *Life in the Trinity.* Downers Grove, IL: InterVarsity Press Academic, 2009.

Feinberg, Charles. *The Minor Prophets*. Chicago, IL: Moody Press, 1977.

Ferguson, Everett. *Church History: Volume I*. Grand Rapids, MI: Zondervan, 2005.

Finke, Roger, and Rodney Stark. *The Churching of America 1776–1990*. New Brunswick, NJ: Rutgers University Press, 1993.

Finley, Thomas. *Joel, Amos, Obadiah: An Exegetical Commentary*. Biblical Studies Press, 2003.

Flake, Kathleen. *The Politics of American Religious Identity*. Chapel Hill, NC: University of North Carolina Press, 2004.

Fletcher, Allen. *A Study Guide to the Facsimiles of the Book of Abraham*. Springville, UT: Cedar Fort, 2006.

Foster, Lawrence. *Religion and Sexuality: the Shakers, the Mormons and the Oneida Community*. University of Illinois Press, 1984.

———. "The Burned-Over District." In *Encyclopaedia of Millennialism and Millennial Movements*, Edited by Richard Landes, 94–86. New York: Routledge, 2000.

Foster, Paul, ed. *Early Christian Thinkers*. Downers Grove, IL: InterVarsity Press Academic, 2011.

Frame, John. *The Doctrine of God*. Phillipsburg, NJ: P&R Publishing, 2002.

Frend, W.H.C. *The Early Church*. New York, NY: J.B. Lippincott Company, 1966.

Fuller, Robert. *Religious Revolutionaries*. New York: Palgrave MacMillan, 2004.

Gaustad, Edwin. *Faiths of our Fathers: Religion of the New Nation*. San Francisco, CA: Harper & Row, 1987.

———. *A Religious History of America*. San Francisco, CA: Harper Collins, 1990.

Geisler, Norman. *Systematic Theology, Volume 2: God, Creation*. Minneapolis, MN: Bethany House, 2003.

———, and Winfried Corduan. *Philosophy of Religion*. Grand Rapids, MI: Baker Book House Company, 1988.

Gibbs, Josiah. *Lights and Shadows of Mormonism*. Salt Lake City, UT: Salt Lake Tribune Publishing, 1909.

Giles, Kevin. *Jesus and the Father: Modern Evangelicals Reinvent the Doctrine of the Trinity*. Grand Rapids, MI: Zondervan, 2006.

Givens, Terry. *By the Hand of Mormon*. New York: Oxford University Press, 2002.

———. *The Book of Mormon: A Very Short Introduction*. New York: Oxford University Press, 2009.

Gomes, Alan. *Unitarian Universalism*. Grand Rapids, MI: Zondervan, 1998.

———. "Faustus Socinus's A Tract Concerning God, Christ, and the Holy Spirit." *Journal for the International Society of Christian Apologetics* 1(2008):37–58.

Gonzalez, Justo. *The Story of Christianity: Two Volumes*. Peabody, MA: Prince Press, 1999.

Green, Bradley, ed. *Shapers of Christian Orthodoxy*. Downers Grove, IL: InterVarsity Press Academic, 2010.

Gregory of Nyssa. "On Not Three Gods," in Vol. 5 of *The Nicene and Post-Nicene Fathers: Second Series*, edited by Phillip Schaff, 326–342. Peabody, MA: Hendrickson Publishers, 2004.

Grudem, Wayne. *Systematic Theology: An Introduction to Biblical Doctrine*. Grand Rapids, MI: Zondervan, 1994.

Gutek, Gerald and Patricia Gutek. *Visiting Utopian Communities*. Columbia, SC: University of South Carolina Press, 1998.

Gutjahr, Paul. *The Book of Mormon: A Biography*. Princeton, NJ: Princeton University Press, 2012.

Hale, Van. "Defining the Contemporary Mormon Concept of God." In *Line Upon Line: Essays on Mormon Doctrine* Edited by Gary Bergera, 7–14. Salt Lake City, UT: Signature Books, 1989.

Hanson, R.P.C. *The Search for the Christian Doctrine of God.* Grand Rapids, MI: Baker Academic, 2006.

Hardy, Grant, ed. *The Book of Mormon: A Reader's Edition.* University of Illinois Press, 2005.

Harrison, R.K. *Introduction to the Old Testament.* Grand Rapids, MI: Eerdmans, 1969.

Hatch, Nathan. "The Origins of Civil Millennialism in America." In *Reckoning the Past.* Edited by D.G. Hart, 85–17. Grand Rapids, MI: Baker Book House, 1995. Originally published in *The William and Mary Quarterly* 3(1974):407–430.

———. *The Democratization of American Christianity.* New Haven, CT: Yale University Press, 1989.

Haykin, Michael. *Rediscovering the Church Fathers.* Wheaton, IL: Crossway Publishers, 2011.

Heschel, Abraham. *The Prophets.* Peabody, MA: Hendrickson Publishing, 2007.

Higgins, Peter. *Numbers: A Very Short Introduction.* New York: Oxford University Press, 2011.

Hinckley, Gordon. *The Teachings of Gordon B. Hinckley.* Salt Lake City, UT: Deseret Books, 1997.

Holmes, David. *The Faiths of the Founding Fathers.* New York: Oxford University Press, 2006.

Hopkins, Richard. *Biblical Mormonism.* Springville, UT: Horizon Book Publishers, 1994.

Horrell, Scott. "The Eternal Son of God in the Social Trinity." In *Jesus in Trinitarian Perspective,* edited by Klaus Issler and Fred Sanders, 44–79. Nashville, TN: Broadman & Holman Academic, 2007.

Horton, Michael. *The Christian Faith.* Grand Rapids, MI: Zondervan, 2011.

Howe, Daniel. *What Hath God Wrought: The Transformation of America, 1815–1848.* New York: Oxford University Press, 2007.

Hill, Jonathon. *The History of Christian Thought.* Downers Grove, IL: InterVarsity Press, 2003.

———. *Zondervan Handbook to the History of Christianity.* Grand Rapids, MI: Zondervan, 2006.

Hudson, David. *History of Jemima Wilkinson.* Geneva, NY: S.P. Hull, 1821.

Hunter, Milton. *The Gospel Through the Ages.* Stevens and Wallis, 1945.

Hurtado, Larry. *One God, One Lord: Early Christian Devotion and Ancient Jewish Monotheism.* Philadelphia, PA: Fortress Press, 1996.

———. *Lord Jesus Christ: Devotion to Jesus in Earliest Christianity.* Grand Rapids, MI: Eerdmans, 2002.

Hyde, Orson. *Journal of Discourses,* 1853. No pages. Online: http://contentdm.lib.byu. edu/cdm/ compoundobject/collection/JournalOfDiscourses3/id/9599/rec/1

Ignatius. "Letter to the Magnesians," in Vol. 9 of *The Ante-Nicene Fathers,* edited by Allan Menzies, 59–65. Peabody, MA: Hendrickson Publishers, 2004.

Irenaeus. "Against Heresies," in Vol. 1 of *The Ante- Nicene Fathers,* edited by Alexander Roberts and James Donaldson, 309–567. Peabody, MA: Hendrickson Publishers, 2004.

———. 2010. *The Demonstration of the Apostolic Preaching.* Translated by Joseph Robinson. Amazon Digital Services. 137 p.

Issler, Klaus, and Fred Sanders, *eds. Jesus in Trinitarian Perspective*. Nashville, TN: Broadman & Holman Academic, 2007.

Jenkins, Philip. *Mystics and Messiahs*. New York: Oxford University Press, 2000.

Jeremias, Jorg. *The Prayers of Jesus*. Philadelphia, PA: Fortress Press, 1989.

———. 1998. *The Book of Amos*. Philadelphia, PA: John Knox Press. 200 p.

Jessee, Dean. *The Papers of Joseph Smith: Vol. 1*. Salt Lake City, UT: Deseret Books, 1989.

———. *The Papers of Joseph Smith: Vol. 2*. Salt Lake City, UT: Deseret Books, 1992.

Johnston, Sarah. *Religions of the Ancient World*. Harvard University Press, 2004.

Justin Martyr. "Dialogue with Trypho," in Vol. 9 of *The Ante-Nicene Fathers* edited Allan Menzies, 194–270. Peabody, MA: Hendrickson Publishers, 2004.

———. "First Apology," in Vol. 9 of *The Ante-Nicene Fathers* edited Allan Menzies, 159–187. Peabody, MA: Hendrickson Publishers, 2004.

Kauffman, Ruth, and Reginald Kauffman. *The Latter Day Saints*. University of Illinois Press, 1912.

Kaiser, Walter. *The Promise-Plan of God: A Biblical Theology of the Old and New Testaments*. Grand Rapids, MI: Zondervan, 2008.

Keener, Craid. *The IVP Bible Background Commentary: New Testament*. Downers Grove, IL: InterVarsity Press, 1993.

Kelly, J.N.D. *Early Christian Doctrines*. New York, NY: Harper & Brothers Publishers, 1960.

Kidd, Thomas. *The Great Awakening*. Yale University Press, 2007.

———. *God of Liberty*. New York: Basic Books, 2010.

Kirkland, Boyd. "The Development of the Mormon Doctrine of God." In *Line Upon Line: Essays on Mormon Doctrine* Edited by Gary Bergera, 35–49. Salt Lake City, UT: Signature Books, 1989.

Kitagawa, Joseph. *The History of Religions*. Oxford University Press, 1987.

Korpel, Marjo. *A Rift in the Clouds: Ugaritic and Hebrew Descriptions of the Divine*. Ugarit-Verlag, 1990.

Köstenberger, Andreas. *A Theology of John's Gospel and Letters*. Grand Rapids, MI: Zondervan, 2009.

———, and Scott Swain. *Father, Son and Spirit: The Trinity and John's Gospel*. Downers Grove, IL: InterVarsity Press, 2008.

Lambert, Frank. *Founding Fathers and the Place of Religion in America*. Princeton, NJ: Princeton University Press, 2003.

Landes, Richard, *ed. Encyclopaedia of Millennialism and Millennial Movements*. New York: Routledge, 2000.

Latourette, Kenneth. *A History of Christianity: Volume I*. Peabody, MA: Prince Press, 2007.

———. *A History of Christianity: Volume II*. Peabody, MA: Prince Press, 2007.

Letham, Robert. *The Holy Trinity*. Phillipsburg,NJ: P&R Publishing, 2004.

Liftin, Bryan. "Origen." In *Shapers of Christian Orthodoxy*, edited by Bradley Green, 108–152. Grove, IL: InterVarsity Press Academic, 2010.

Lightner, Robert. *The God of the Bible*. Grand Rapids, MI: Baker, 1978.

Lohse, Bernhard. *A Short History of Christian Doctrine*. Philadelphia, PA: Fortress Press, 1985.

Lohse, Eduard. *The New Testament Environment*. Nashville, TN: Abingdon, 1988.

Ludlow, Daniel, *ed. Encyclopaedia of Mormonism*. Salt Lake City, UT: Deseret Books, 1992.

Lyman, Rebecca. "Origen." In *Early Christian Thinkers*, edited by Paul Foster, 111–126. Downers Grove, IL: InterVarsity Press Academic, 2011.

Marsh, J, ed. 2005. *The Eyewitness History of the Church, Volume One: The Restoration, 1800–1833.* Springville, UT: Cedar Fort, 2005.

Maspero, Giulio. *Trinity and Man: Gregory of Nyssa's Ad Ablabium.* The Netherlands: Brill, 2007.

Mathisen, Robert, ed. *Critical Issues in American Religious History.* Waco, TX: Baylor University Press, 2006.

Matthews, Kenneth. *NAC Volume 1: Genesis 1–11.* Nashville, TN: Broadman & Holman, 1996.

Matthews, Victor. *Old Testament Turning Points.* Grand Rapids, MI: Baker Academic, 2005.

Mays, James. *Amos.* Philadelphia, PA: John Knox Press, 1969.

McComiskey, Thomas. "Amos" in Vol. 7 of *The Expositor's Bible Commentary,* edited by Frank Gaebelein, 269–334. Grand Rapids, MI: Zondervan, 1984.

McConkie, Bruce. *Mormon Doctrine.* Salt Lake City, UT: Bookcraft, 1979.

———. 1984. The Caravan Moves On. *Ensign Magazine.* 82 p.

———. *Doctrinal Commentary on the New Testament: Volume 3.* Salt Lake City, UT: Bookcraft, 1998.

McConkie, Joseph, and Robert Millet. *Doctrinal Commentary on the Book of Mormon: Volume I.* Salt Lake City, UT: Bookcraft, 1987.

McDonald, Lee. *The Biblical Canon.* Peabody, MA: Hendrickson, 2007.

McGrath, Alister. *Understanding Doctrine.* Grand Rapids, MI: Zondervan, 1990.

———. *Heresy.* New York: HarperOne, 2009.

———. *Christian Theology: An Introduction.* United Kingdom: John Wiley & Sons Ltd, 2011.

McKim, Donald, ed. *Dictionary of Major Biblical Interpreters.* Downer Grove, IL: InterVarsity Press Academic, 2007.

McLoughlin, William. "The Role of Religion in the Revolution." In *Critical Issues in American Religious History,* edited by Robert Mathisen, 148–153. Waco, TX: Baylor University Press, 2006.

Miles, Todd. *A God of Many Understandings?* Nashville, TN: B&H Academic, 2010.

Millet, Robert. "The Eternal Gospel," *Ensign Magazine,* July, 1996.

———. *The Mormon Faith.* Shadow Mountain Press, 1998.

———. "What is Our Doctrine?" *The Religious Educator* 4 (2003):15–33.

———. *A Different Jesus?* Grand Rapids, MI: Eerdmans Publishing, 2005.

———, and Noel Reynolds. *Latter-day Christianity.* Provo, UT: FARMS, 1998.

———, & Gerald McDermott. *Claiming Christ.* Grand Rapids, MI: Brazo Press, 2007.

Mills, Watson, and Richard Wilson, eds. *Mercer Commentary on the Bible.* Macon, GA: Mercer University Press, 1995.

Minns, Denis. *Irenaeus: An Introduction.* New York, NY: T&T Clark, 2010.

———. "Irenaeus." In *Early Christian Thinkers,* edited by Paul Foster, 36–51.Downers Grove, IL: InterVarsity Press Academic, 2011.

Moody, Dale. "God's Only Son: The Translation of John 3:16 in the Revised Standard Version." *The Journal of Biblical Literature,* 4(1953):214.

Morgan, Edward. *The Incarnation of the Word: The Theology of Augustine of Hippo.* New York, NY: T&T Clark International, 2010.

Moreland, J.P. *Scaling the Secular City.* Grand Rapids, MI: Baker Book House, 1987.

Morris, Leon. *New Testament Theology.* Grand Rapids, MI: Zondervan, 1990.

———. *NICNT: The Gospel According to John.* Grand Rapids, MI: Eerdmans, 1995.

Bibliography

Mounce, William. *Mounce's Complete Expository dictionary of Old Testament and New Testament Words*. Grand Rapids, MI: Zondervan, 2006.

Neusner, Jacob. *Judaism When Christianity Began*. Louisville, KY: John Knox Press, 2002.

Newman, Sharan. *The Real History of the End of the World*. New York: Berkley Books, 2010.

Newport, Kenneth, and Crawford Gribben, eds. *Expecting the End: Millennialism in Social and Historical Context*. Waco, TX: Baylor University Press, 2006.

Newell, Linda, and Valeen Avery. *Mormon Enigma: Emma Hale Smith*. Champaign, IL: University of Illinois Press, 1994.

Nibley, Hugh. *The Message of the Joseph Smith Papyri*. Salt Lake City, UT: Deseret Book Company, 2005. Noll, K.L. *Canaan and Israel in Antiquity*. Lexington, NY: Continuum International Publishing Group, 2001.

Noll, Mark. *A History of Christianity in the United States and Canada*. Grand Rapids, MI: Eerdmans, 1992.

———. *America's God*. New York, NY: Oxford University Press, 2005.

———. *The Rise of Evangelicalism*. Downers Grove, IL: InterVarsity Press, 2010.

Oaks, Dallin. "Apostasy and Restoration," *Ensign Magazine*, May, 1995.

Oakes, Peter. *Philippians: From People to Letter*. Cambridge: Cambridge University Press, 2001.

O'Brien, Peter. *The New International Greek Testament Commentary: Philippians*. Grand Rapids, MI: Eerdmans, 1991.

Olson, Roger, and Christopher Hall. *The Trinity*. Grand Rapids, MI: Eerdmans, 2002.

Oman, Nathan. "Jurisprudence and the Problem of Church Doctrine." *Element: Journal of the Society for Mormon Philosophy and Theology* 2(2006):1–19.

Oppy, Graham. *Philosophical Perspectives on Infinity*. Cambridge University Press, 2006.

Origen.*The Early Christians Fathers: Origen's Commentary on Romans*. Translated by Henry Bettenson. London: Oxford University Press, 1969.

———. 1989. *Origen's Commentary on the Gospel According to John*. Translated by Ronald Heine. Catholic University Press. 327 p.

———. "On First Principles," in Vol. 4 of *The Ante- Nicene Fathers* edited by Alexander Roberts and James Donaldson, 239–284. Peabody, MA: Hendrickson Publishers, 2004.

Osborn, Eric. *Irenaeus of Lyons*. New York, NY: Cambridge University Press, 2001.

———. *Tertullian: First Theologian of the West*. New York, NY: Cambridge University Press, 2003.

Oswalt, John. *The New International Commentary on the Old Testament: The Book of Isaiah*. Grand Rapids, MI: Eerdmans Publishing, 1998.

———. *The Bible Among the Myths*. Grand Rapids, MI: Zondervan, 2009.

Paul, Shalom, and Frank Cross, eds. *Amos*. Philadelphia, PA: Fortress Press, 1991.

Pelikan, Jaroslav. *The Emergence of the Catholic Tradition (100–600)*. Chicago, IL: Chicago University Press, 1975.

Persuitte, David. *Joseph Smith and the Origins of the Book of Mormon*. Jefferson, NC: McFarland & Company Publishers, 2000.

Peterson, Daniel, and Stephen Ricks. "Comparing LDS Beliefs with First-Century Christianity," *Ensign Magazine*, March, 1988.

———. *Offenders for a Word*. Provo, UT: FARMS, 1998.

Peterson, H.D. *Moroni: Ancient Prophet, Modern Messenger*. Springville, UT: Cedar Fort, 2008.

———. *The Story of the Book of Abraham*. Springville, UT: Cedar Fort, 2008.

Pojman, Louis, *ed. Philosophy of Religion*. Belmont, CA: Wadsworth Publishing House, 1998.

Pratt, Parley. *Key to the Science of Theology*. Salt Lake City, UT: Deseret Books, 1893.

Preuss, Horst. *Old Testament Theology: Volume I*. Louisville, KY: John Knox Press, 1995.

———. *Old Testament Theology: Volume II*. Louisville, KY: John Knox Press, 1996.

Quash, Ben, Michael Ward, *eds. Heresies and How to Avoid Them*. Peabody, MA: Hendrickson Publishing, 2007.

Quinn, D.M. *Early Mormonism and the Magic World View*. Salt Lake City, UT: Signature Books, 1998.

Reeves, Michael. *Delighting in the Trinity*. Downers Grove, IL: IVP Academic, 2012.

Remini, Robert. *Joseph Smith*. New York, NY: Viking Adult, 2002.

Reynolds, George. *The Story of the Book of Mormon*. Salt Lake City, UT: Press of Geo. Q. Cannon & Sons Co, 1898.

———, and Janne Sjodahl. *Commentary on the Book of Mormon*. Salt Lake City, UT: Deseret Book, 1976.

Rhodes, Michael. "A Translation and Commentary of the Joseph Smith Hypocephalus." *Brigham Young University Studies* 17 (1977):265.

Richardson, Cyril, *ed. Early Christian Fathers*. Louisville, KY: John Knox Press, 2006.

Riley, Woodbridge. *The Founder of Mormonism: A Psychological Study of Joseph Smith*. New York: Dodd, Mead & Company, 1902.

Roberts, B.H., *ed. History of the Church: Volume 6*. Salt Lake City, UT: Deseret Books, 1980.

Roberts, R.P. *Mormonism Unmasked*. Nashville, TN: B&H Books, 1998.

Robinson, Stephen. *Are Mormons Christians?* Salt Lake City, UT: Bookcraft, 1991.

Rofe, Alexander. *Old Testament Studies: Deuteronomy*. New York: T&T Clark, 2002.

Rogers Jr., Cleon, and Cleon Rogers III. *The New Linguistic and Exegetical Key to the Greek New Testament*. Grand Rapids, MI: Zondervan, 1998.

Robbins, Caroline. *The Eighteenth Century Commonwealthman*. New York: Antheneum, 1968.

Rusch, William. *The Trinitarian Controversy*. Philadelphia, PA: Fortress Press, 1980.

Ryken, Philip, and Michael LeFebvre. *Our Triune God*. Wheaton, IL: Crossway, 2011.

Ryrie, Charles. *Basic Theology*. Chicago, IL: Moody Press, 1996.

Sailhamer, John. *The Pentateuch as Narrative: A Biblical-Theological Commentary*. Grand Rapids, MI: Zondervan, 1992.

Sanders, Fred. *The Deep Things of God*. Wheaton, IL: Crossway, 2010.

Sandoz, Ellis. *Republicanism, Religion, and the Soul of America*. Columbia, MO: University of Missouri Press, 2006.

Scott, Julius. *Jewish Backgrounds of the New Testament*. Grand Rapids, MI: Baker Academic, 2006.

Schreiner, Thomas. *New Testament Theology*. Grand Rapids, MI: Baker Academic, 2008.

Shedd, W.T. *Dogmatic Theology*. Phillipsburg, NJ: P&R Publishing, 2003.

Shelton, Brian. "Irenaeus." In *Shapers of Christian Orthodoxy*, edited by Bradley Green, 15–63. Downers Grove, IL: InterVarsity Press Academic, 2010.

Silva, Moises. *Biblical Words and Their Meaning*. Grand Rapids, MI: Zondervan, 1995.

———. *Philippians: BECNT*. Grand Rapids, MI: Baker Academic, 2008.

Sire, James. *The Universe Next Door*. Downers Grove, IL: InterVarsity Press Academic, 2009.

Bibliography

Skousen, Cleon. *The First Two-Thousand Years*. Salt Lake City, UT: Bookcraft, 1953.

Smith, Elias. *The Life, Conversion, Preaching, Travels, and Sufferings of Elias Smith: Volume I*. Boston, MA, 1840.

Smith, Hyrum, and Janne Sjodahl. *Doctrine and Covenants Commentary*. Salt Lake City, UT: Deseret Books, 1923.

Smith, Joseph, F. *Teachings of the Prophet Joseph Smith*. CreateSpace, 2009.

Smith, Joseph. *Journal of Discourse*, 1844. No pages. Online: http://contentdm.lib.byu.edu/cdm/%20compoundobject/collection/JournalOfDiscourses3/id/9602/rec/6

———. 1844. *Times and Seasons*. Volume 5(15): 613–615.

———. *History of Joseph Smith: The Prophet, by Himself*. Salt Lake City, UT: Deseret Books, 1902.

———., trans. *Book of Mormon*. Salt Lake City, UT: The Church of Jesus Christ Latter-day Saints, 1948.

———. *The Personal Writings of Joseph Smith*. Edited by Dean Jessee. Salt Lake City, UT: Deseret Books, 2002.

Smith, Lucy. *Biographical Sketches of Joseph Smith, the Prophet*. Liverpool: S.W. Richards, 1853.

Smith, Mark. *God in Translation: Deities in Cross-Cultural Discourse in the Biblical World*. Grand Rapids, MI: Eerdmans, 2010.

Smither, Edward. *Augustine as Mentor*. Nashville, TN: B&H Academic, 2008.

Soskice, Janet. "Biblical Trinitarianism." In *Heresies and How to Avoid Them*, edited by Ben Quash and Michael Ward, 122–130. Peabody, MA: Hendrickson Publishing, 2007.

Spitzer, Robert. *New Proofs for the Existence of God*. Grand Rapids, MI: Eerdmans, 2010.

Stack, P.F. "Apostle Says Key to LDS Beliefs is Divine Revelation." *Salt Lake City Tribune*: 1 April. 2012. http://www.sltrib.com/sltrib/news/53833402–78/church-mormon-apostlelds.html.csp

Stein, Stephen. *Communities of Dissent: A History of Alternative Religions in America*. New York: Oxford University Press, 2003.

Stone, Jon. "Nineteenth and Twentieth-Century American Millennialism." In *The Oxford Handbook of Millennialism*, edited by Catherine Wessinger, 492–495. New York: Oxford University Press, 2011.

Strecker, Georg. *Theology of the New Testament*. Louisville, KY: John Knox Press, 2000.

Stuckenbruck, Loren, and Wendy Sproston North. *Early Jewish and Christian Monotheism*. New York: T&T Clark International, 2004.

Stump, Eleonore, and Norman Kretzmann, eds. *The Cambridge Companion to Augustine*. New York, NY: Cambridge University Press, 2001.

Sweeney, Marvin, ed. *The Twelve Prophets*. Collegeville, MN: Liturgical Press, 2000.

Sweet, William. *The Story of Religion in America*. Grand Rapids, MI: Baker Book House, 1973.

Talmage, James. *The Articles of Faith*. Salt Lake City, UT: Deseret Books, 1899.

———. *The Great Apostasy*. Salt Lake City, UT: Deseret Books, 1909.

———. *Jesus the Christ*. Salt Lake City, UT: Deseret Books, 1916.

Tennent, Timothy. *Christianity at the Religious Roundtable*. Grand Rapids, MI: Baker Academic, 2002.

Tenney, Merrill. "John," in Vol. 9 of *The Expositor's Bible Commentary*, edited by Frank Gaebelein, 3–206. Grand Rapids, MI: Zondervan, 1981.

Tertullian. "Against Praxaes," in Vol. 3 of *The Ante- Nicene Fathers*, edited by Alexander Roberts and James Donaldson, 597–632. Peabody, MA: Hendrickson Publishers, 2004.

———. "Apology," Vol. 3 of *The Ante- Nicene Fathers*, edited by Alexander Roberts and James Donaldson, 17–60. Peabody, MA: Hendrickson Publishers, 2004.

The First Presidency. *True to the Faith*. Salt Lake City, UT: The Church of Jesus Christ of Latter-day Saints, 2004.

Thielman, Frank. *Theology of the New Testament*. Grand Rapids, MI: Zondervan, 2005.

Theissen, Henry. *Lectures in Systematic Theology*. Grand Rapids, MI: Eerdmans, 1990.

Torrance, Thomas. *Trinitarian Perspectives*. Edinburgh, Scotland: T&T Clark, 1994.

———. *The Christian Doctrine of God*. Edinburgh, Scotland: T&T Clark, 1996.

Tucker, Pomeroy. *Origin, Rise and Progress of Mormonism*. Broadway, NY: D. Appleton and Company, 1867.

Tucker, Ruth. *Another Gospel*. Grand Rapids, MI: Zondervan, 2004.

Tullidge, Edward. *The Life of Joseph the Prophet*. Salt Lake City, UT: Publisher's Press, 1878.

Vanhoozer, Kevin. *First Theology*. Downers Grove, IL: InterVarsity Press, 2002.

———, ed. *Dictionary for Theological Interpretation of the Bible*. Grand Rapids, MI: Baker Academic, 2005.

Verbrugge, Verlyn. *New International Dictionary of New Testament Theology*. Grand Rapids, MI: Zondervan, 2003.

Vogel, Dan. "The Earliest Mormon Concept of God." In *Line Upon Line: Essays on Mormon Doctrine*, edited by Gary Bergera, 17–33. Salt Lake City, UT: Signature Books, 1989.

Walton, John. *Ancient Near Eastern Thought in the Old Testament*. Grand Rapids, MI: Baker Book House, 2006.

———, ed. *Zondervan Illustrated Bible Backgrounds Commentary*. Grand Rapid, MI: Zondervan, 2009.

———, Victor Matthews, and Mark Chavalas. *The IVP Background Commentary* of the Old Testament. Downers Grove, IL: InterVarsity Press, 2000.

Walvoord, John. *The Holy Spirit*. Grand Rapids, MI: Zondervan, 1991.

Warfield, B.B. *The Works of Benjamin Breckinridge Warfield: Volume II*. Grand Rapids, MI: Baker, 1981.

Wessinger, Catherine, ed. *The Oxford Handbook of Millennialism*. New York: Oxford University Press, 2011.

Westermann, Claus. *Genesis 1–11: A Commentary*. Minneapolis: Augsburg Publishing House, 1994.

White, James. *Is the Mormon My Brother?* Minneapolis, MN: Bethany House, 1997.

———. *The Forgotten Trinity*. Minneapolis, MN. Bethany House, 1998.

White, Kendall. *Mormon Neo-Orthodoxy*. Salt Lake City, UT: Signature Books, 1987.

Wisbey, Herbert. *Pioneer Prophetess*. Cornell University Press, 2009.

Wolf, Herbert. *Interpreting Isaiah*. Grand Rapids, MI: Zondervan Academic, 1985.

Wolffe, John. *The Expansion of Evangelicalism*. Downers Grove, IL: InterVarsity Press, 2007.

Wood, Leon. *The Prophets of Israel*. Grand Rapids, MI: Baker Books, 1998.

Wright, N.T. *The New Testament and the People of God*. Philadelphia, PA: Fortress Press, 1996.

Young, Brigham. *Journal of Discourses*, 1859. No pages. Online: http://contentdm.lib.byu.edu/ cdm/compoundobject/collection/JournalOfDiscourses3/id/9603/rec/7

Bibliography

Young, Edward. *The Book of Isaiah: Volume III*. Grand Rapids, MI: Eerdmans Publishing, 1997.

Zimmerli, Walther. *Old Testament Theology in Outline*. Louisville, KY: John Knox Press, 2000.